Worship In A World Of Excess

Establishing the Priesthood of the Believer

I0098278

By Darren T. Carter

Foundation Publications

www.FoundationPub.org

Worship In A World Of Excess

Establishing the Priesthood of the Believer

INTRODUCTION

Worship In An Age of Excess is the second book in a three-volume series called "**Foundations For Life'**. The series corresponds with the workbook **Building Your Spiritual House**. The second section of *Building Your Spiritual House* is **Created Unto Good Works,** which focuses upon understanding worship regarding being a part of the New Covenant kingdom of priests. The purpose of this book is to make sure we are established in a foundational understanding of worship and the battle the body of Christ will face at the end of the age. At the same time, I hope to help us embrace a balanced view of the priesthood which includes both the inward power of Christ produced through worship and an outward expression of that life demonstrated by good works.

The series 'Foundations for Life' does not have to be read in order, but it will greatly benefit you to read *'Running the Race to Win'* prior to this book. I am building on top of previous teaching, and it is best if the books are followed in sequence. It will also be beneficial for you to use the workbook *'Building Your Spiritual House'* as an additional supplement to study. (Get your free copy: www.FoundationPub.org). The goal of this book is to lay biblical foundations concerning the subject of worship, which the believer can build upon. It is truth that is simple, attainable and applicable, moving us beyond intellectual assent to application, which transforms our character and manner of life.

Daily we have a myriad of images and activities vying for our attention. Modern society moves at a frantic pace leaving far too many of us clinging on to just make it through the day. Have you ever felt like you were continually bowing to the pressures that you face daily and allowing them to master you? Contemporary culture is driven by the desire to possess. Even many in the body of Christ have surrendered to the idea that the good life is found in the accumulation of possessions, power, prestige or pleasure we can attain in this age. It is a consumerist culture that affects every detail of our lives whether we fully understand it or not.

External and internal pressure is nothing new, but modern society with its constant media bombardment and frantic pace of life has produced a level of mental manipulation never encountered. The best way to describe what is happening is that we are being pushed and manipulated into excessive behavior. We see this in all parts of society all around the globe. It is easy to spot this excess in entertainment, politics, sports, sexual behavior, consumerist living, indulgent eating and even religious zeal.

It seems to a lot of people that the Bible is out of date and does not address our modern culture. In this book I want to look at some of the modern phenomenon transforming our world and how as New Covenant priests we are to navigate through this present age. I hope to help us realize that there is only one place to truly live an overcoming life and that is to learn to live life in the liberty of the Spirit. We are called to live a life in union with Christ by His Spirit and to live in this world ministering as a priest bringing restoration to a hurting world.

The book of Revelation was written to the early church, helping it to respond to the predicament in which it was found. The book also addresses the church throughout history and presents a view, which extends to the consummation of this present age and beyond. The writing of this book is in no way an attempt to be a comprehensive study on the book of Revelation. However, I would like to take the main theme of worship and make an application to living as a disciple during these times in which we find ourselves.

As I was living in New York City I frequently went to the park in College Point, Queens across from LaGuardia Airport on Flushing Bay and prayed. I would pray as flights came in and flew out to points around the globe. At the same time, you could see the tall buildings on the island of Manhattan, which most people call "The City". It is the belief of many people that New York City is the powerful city, Babylon, spoken of in the book of Revelation. I do not take that position; however, the spiritual forces shown to be at work in the book of Revelation are at work in influential New York City. The lure of "The City" has been the destruction of many lives as they have chased after sensuality, wealth, prestige and power.

The details of the book of John's Revelation can be confusing and speculative; however, there is a clear message that reoccurs throughout the book. In this book, I want to focus on what I call the major theme of the book of Revelation and that is the theme of worship. Worship can be boiled down to that which you give your life tool. The Spirit does not just want one part of your life, but all parts of your heart and every facet of your life is to be consecrated or set apart for the Spirit of God.

As in my first book, this writing is my personal journey as being one of Christ's disciples. I am a co-pilgrim with you and simply want all that God wants for my life. I have met many co-pilgrims who seem to be on the same journey.

The cry of the heart is that we want to experience Jesus and not just read some old storybook. We want the dynamic, life-giving Christ who cast out demons and used His words to cut to the heart of the matter. We want to see the church as a living organism and not a religious organization.

What happened during the Protestant Reformation that caused such dramatic change in the way people worshiped, which changed society itself? A stirring among the people was happening before Martin Luther nailed his 'Ninety-Five Theses' up. He was nothing but a spark on dry kindling which was ready to burst into flames. It was the fullness of times for that age or period of history.

Martin Luther was simply a prophetic voice discerning the times in which he was living. He saw corruption and idolatry, but he was by no means alone. The masses could not define it, but they were experiencing it. Martin Luther put voice to what people were experiencing. Have you ever felt like something was wrong, but you could not put words to it? Then you heard a word, which defined what you were feeling which brought understanding? Martin Luther did just that for the masses.

One author has clearly articulated that every 500 years God has a rummage sale. We are going through such a time in our day. The last one happened during the 1500's, which we called the Protestant Reformation. Since the early 1900's the church has been going through a 'great transitional cycle', which a few authors have defined as 'Restoration Theology'. Greg Ogden in his book "Unfinished Business" says:

[1] "Nearly five hundred years after the Reformation, there are rumblings in the church that appear to be creating a climate for something so powerful that we can call it a New Reformation. The New Reformation seeks nothing less than the radical

transformation of the self-perception of all believers so that we see ourselves as vital channels through whom God mediates His life to other members of the body of Christ and to the world."

We can look at the history of the church to see that anytime there is a stirring and the Spirit is rearranging or realigning things; it can get messy. Look at the patterns of scripture and you will see when God was bringing monumental change, it usually came in a whirlwind of judgment and restoration. You say, 'I want a move of the Spirit', but I will pass on the things that challenge my thinking and traditions. Yes, we all have them!

Traditions are just established norms, and we all have our traditions, which may not necessarily be bad unless they keep us from serving Christ with all our hearts. It is wise to remember Jesus' first miracle (John 2:1-11) was to take six stone water jars used for ceremonial washing and make good wine. Jesus is still in the business of transformation! He can take rigid ritualistic systems and give them new life.

I am making an appeal in the introduction of this book to openness. It is an appeal to flexibility, which worship demands if we are too do it in spirit and truth. Worship is not bound to any particular tradition or church structure. This book does not advocate for any specific worship style, tradition, or interpretation of the book of Revelation. Instead, it encourages readers to devote themselves to the God who created heaven and earth, Jesus Christ. We have far too long divided over trivial matters such as worship style and our particular interpretation of Revelation. I am not saying to disregard either, but I am saying that the Father is not overly concerned about such things.

Globally, there is a shift in the way religious practices are conducted. Many individuals now practice their beliefs outside of the traditional church setting. Multitudes are serving through marketplace ministries, house church networks, simple church and many alternative forms of fellowship and outreach. [2] "The church is being released from its institutional entrapment and is rediscovering its primary identity as a living body. The church as organism suggests that God's people are indwelled with the presence of the living Christ."

In the book of Acts, you see the *micro church* meeting primarily in homes and the *macro church* or large gatherings of believers. Our unity is not found in conforming to one another's structures, but our common fellowship with the one resurrected Christ. It is going to take every part of the body to work together to fulfill our mission. We may not have common structures, traditions, or practices, but we have a common union in Christ.

We have had renewal movements, but never the radical transition of how we *practice our faith* as we are in the middle of right now. The transition seems to be a reversal of what happened in the book of I Samuel 8. In this portion of scripture, the Israelites demanded a king so that they could be like the other nations. It was not God's intent! He wanted them to be a 'kingdom of priests' that had God as their King and not look to someone else to neither direct their lives nor approach God on their behalf. Personal responsibility is the key to transformation where Christ becomes our head.

[3] "In order for the priesthood of all believers to be a reality, we must experience the church as a living organism. The church that is a living extension of Jesus values all parts of the body without any hierarchy of status given to the parts. Jesus is free to run His church, and it comes alive to the indwelling presence of Christ when all the parts of the body seek to know their valued place in the body of Christ."

The New Covenant is about the believer having a personal relationship with God and fulfilling the purpose of God for their individual lives. As a 'kingdom of priests' everyone has a responsibility; to take their place in using their gifts, in serving one another and a needy world. The priesthood of the believer refers to the concept that each member of a community has an individual responsibility to act as a priest before God and to minister to others. It highlights the idea that a community consists of individual believers who have committed themselves to serving others.

The church has been experiencing a transition, and this transition is bringing a 'radical' new way of being the household of faith and a 'radical' new way of serving as one of Christ "servant leaders". It is not new, but a return to Biblical mandates as to how we practice our faith and exercise our leadership in the church and the world.

The word radical comes from the Latin word radix, which

means 'root'. So, to be radical is to get down to the root of things, penetrating its essence and not being distracted by the many sidetracks. The root of our service to God and others is learning to be a servant, which exemplifies who we worship. If we are experiencing vertical worship with our Father then we are going to display the heart of the Son of God, which is the heart of a servant. Serving is a practical expression of the Father's love through a heart of worship.

It would be easy to take what I am saying out of context and say I am talking about having no functioning leadership. I am not! We are equally one in Christ; however, there are different levels of authority and structure within a community. Not everyone within the community has the same authority, purpose and abilities (I Corinthians 12:12-29; Romans 12:3-16).

The substructure of the organism, which we call the church are **a**postles, **p**rophets, **e**vangelists, **s**hepherds and **t**eachers (Ephesians 4:11). What is called the APEST gifts are not authoritative offices in a hierarchical structure, but gifts used to build up and equip to body of Christ to grow. You can get more information about this subject if you go to www.foundationpub.org Lesson 49: Equipping The Saints.

On a local level we have elders who are assigned to oversee and instruct (Acts 20:28; I Peter 5:2) along with those who serve with them, which I Timothy 3:8 calls deacons (managers) or 'organizational servants'. In I Timothy 3:1-14 we can see that there are character qualifications which are required for holding one of these leadership positions, which gives them a greater responsibility to the greater community and to God (James 3:1; I Timothy 5:20).

The character qualifications of leadership cannot be compromised, but I am not going to put strict definitions on an exact structural form of leadership that must adhere to. I will say that simplicity and flexibility are of necessity. (To get more details on this subject go to Lessons 45-50 in the book 'Building Your Spiritual House' www.FoundationPub.org.)

The point I am making is that we need a functioning leadership structure to accomplish tasks, but even the leaders are just a part. The purpose of leadership is to help each team member reach their full potential and cause the team members to accomplish their God given purpose. We need sacrificial "servant leaders" who will pour out their lives to make sure others find their purpose.

Leadership is for the purpose of undergirding and supporting others, not the other way around. Service captures the spirit in which our leadership is to be rendered on behalf of others.

True worship is about abiding in the life of Christ where mercy and judgment kiss together. True spiritual authority is a result of intimate fellowship with Him who has overcome death, hell and the grave. We cannot represent Christ in this earth as His priesthood until we learn to have intimate fellowship with Him. Unless you eat the flesh of Christ and drink His blood you cannot truly represent His heart, life and character.

As we get closer and closer to the end of the age, spiritual winds will be separating the wheat from the tares. In looking at this parable that Jesus used to teach He says the wheat and tares will grow along together in the world until the harvest (Matthew 13:36- 43). When wheat is ready for harvest, the plants at maturity are not very tall, only about 12-15 inches. The tares, on the other hand, keep on growing, poking their unproductive heads four or five inches above the wheat crop making them easy to distinguish. Unlike the tares, mature wheat bows over like worshipping believers, especially apparent at the end of the age.

Numerous authors are identifying what are called the 'signs of the times' and declaring that we are on the precipice of the end of this age. One thing that we need to keep in mind is that we are not the first generation of believers who have thought they would be the generation when Christ would return. It especially becomes an issue when we face hardship during a great turning point in history like the Napoleonic Wars of Europe, the U.S. Civil War, WWI, the Great Depression, WWII with the example of Hitler being an antichrist and even the turmoil during the 1960's drug induced "Sexual Revolution".

Peter in speaking to the first century church said that Christ appeared at the end of times or last days (I Peter 1:20). The early church was living in what we would call the 'last days' which started with the first coming, death, resurrection and ascension of Christ. It found its apex at the destruction of the city of Jerusalem in 70 A.D. when the Jewish Temple was destroyed with the ceasing of the sacrifices that has never returned. However, Christ in Matthew 24 did give us specific signs that would precede the completion of the last days, or the end of the age. History is coming to a climax, and we are told to be aware of the conditions in the world, while at the same time expectant concerning the return of Christ.

Peter said, "Know this first of all, that in the last days mockers will come with their mocking, following after their own lusts, and saying, 'Where is the promise of His coming? For ever since the fathers fell asleep, all continues just as it was from the beginning of creation'" (II Peter 3:3-4). The world mocks the possibility of Christ's return, and many even in the church don't give it much thought. I am not recommending fanaticism, but wisdom is a key for the church at the end of this age.

Wisdom puts things in their proper perspective. Peter recommended three things in reference to the unveiling, revelation or return of Christ that are hope, sober mindedness and action (I Peter 1:13). It is my intent to help us put worship in its proper perspective so that we have hope, stay sober minded and are moved to action as we see history unfold.

In the book of Revelation, we see that the "Spirit of Prophecy" is the testimony of Jesus Christ (Rev. 19:20). He is the sum total of history since He is the Alpha and Omega or Beginning and End of history (Rev. 1:8). At least 332 times the Old Testament prophets predicted that Jesus would come – and in His first coming He fulfilled many of those prophecies. The majority of the Bible's unfulfilled prophecies concern the return of Christ and He will be the summing up of history since it is "His-story".

The book of Daniel correlates with the book of Revelation, and he speaks of the 'Son of Man' in reference to Messiah. Jesus used this statement about Himself and His return (Matt. 24:30). [5]"The Son of Man descended to the cross to bear divine judgment for us and ascended to heaven from where He will rescue us from history's calamities and its erasing of our transitory lives. The salvation He offers is a deliverance from judgment". History is going to find its culmination in Christ and our worship of Him is going to be the separating factor determining if we are overcomers, bearing His divine nature.

Worship will be the separating factor at the end of this age. True worshipers of the Living God have humble obedient hearts to the Spirit of God. However, tares are worshipers of such things like sensuality, wealth, power and religion, with hearts hardened and lifted up in pride. It is my intention through this small book to help you become the worshiping wheat that is going to bow before the sovereign rule of the King of kings.

CHAPTER 1

LIVING LIFE FROM A HEAVENLY VIEW

"You have come to Mount Zion and to the city of the living
God, the heavenly Jerusalem, and to myriads of angels."
~ **Hebrews 12:22**~

It has always been God's desire to bring forth a priesthood
that would be His representatives in the earth. Several authors have
pointed to the biblical evidence that Adam performed priestly
functions while in Eden. Such a conclusion is drawn from the close
parallels between Eden and the later worship centers in
Israel.
    In the book of Genesis, you can find the seeds of the entire
Bible. We see a clear pattern in Eden of God's desires toward man
and it correlates with the later worship centers of Israel. It is merely
symbolic, but it is a biblical pattern. Eden and the worship centers
are both entered from the East and guarded by cherubim (Gen.3:24;
Ex. 25:18-22).
    God walked in communion with man in Eden and in the
worship centers. [1] "The river's flowing out of Eden are matched by
the river flowing from Ezekiel's visionary Temple (Gen. 2:10; Ezekiel
47:1-12)". We even see correlations to the seven-branched
candlestick providing the only light in the holy place to the 'Tree of
Life' in Eden (Gen. 2:9; 3:22; Exodus 25:31- 35). Eden is portrayed
as being on a mountain where the four rivers flowed out and the
later worship centers of Israel are on the top of a hill where the four
winds blow over the threshing floor.
    It has always been the Father's heart to have a faithful
priesthood that would reflect His nature of holiness, mercy, love,
power and impartial judgment. Man was always supposed to be the
image-bearer of the Father's character. One of the aspects of being
made in the image of God is to reflect His character.

God told the children of Israel through Moses that, "you shall be to me a kingdom of priests..." (Exodus 19:6). It is evident that the nation of Israel never fully entered that calling, but the Father has not stopped seeking such a kingdom of priests. We see in the book of Revelation that the Father sees His desires manifest in this age with such a kingdom and priests representing the rule of Christ upon the earth (Rev. 5:10).

It is important that we understand that in Christ we have been called to be a part of His kingdom of priests seated in heavenly places with Him (Ephesians 2:6). I am not talking about some kind of spooky or impractical reality but simply learning to have our complete identification and focus upon Christ who is our victory through faith.

We are a New Covenant people born of the resurrected life of the Spirit. [2] "We have left the realm of the tangible and the natural. We are in the spirit and have come unto Mount Zion, the mountain of grace and truth." Our lives are transformed by the power of the Holy Spirit, but we are also called to practically apply the life of the Spirit to every detail of our lives. Worship is tapping into the transforming power of the cross and the wisdom of applied truth to all areas of our existence.

The book of Revelation speaks of those who overcome through lives dedicated to worshipping. To be the overcomers that we are called to be we must learn to enter the Sabbath rest of heaven. It is the author of Hebrews who paints a word picture for us describing the rest of God.

In the book of Hebrews, we find the author contrasts the earthly ministry of Israel to the heavenly ministry of Christ. He shows us the superiority of the New Covenant and clearly portrays the Old Covenant ministries and promises as having been brought to completion and fulfillment in Christ. The law and prophets have been replaced by the true reality of God in human flesh. The types and shadows, of which they spoke are no longer the focus, because they have been consumed by the brightness of the glory of Christ (II Corinthians 3: 7-18).

We must be found in Christ by stripping ourselves of our own identity and being clothed in His heavenly garments. The garments of the High Priest [3] "were to be made of linen (Exod. 28:6), the purpose of which was so that they would not sweat...Sweat is an element of the curse in Genesis 3:18." We can no longer draw our identity from this present age. We must embrace our heavenly identity resting under the shadow of the cross so that as we pray, prophesy, share our faith, give, praise or work on the job we are wearing the linen garments of grace co-laboring in the life of the Spirit.

The book of Hebrews clearly portrays Christ as our Heavenly High Priest calling us to be seated in heavenly places with Him established in His unshakable kingdom (Hebrews 12:28). If we could pull the curtain back on this world, we would see a very different reality than what we see with our natural eyes, surrounded by a great heavenly host. Sure, there are principalities and powers of darkness, but they know their time is short since; the cross has overpowered them.

We don't yet see all things put under the feet of Christ, but we can be assured that all authority in heaven, on earth and under the earth has been given to Christ (Philippians 2:9- 11). However, for us to be partakers of the cross we must humble ourselves daily under the under the power of the blood, water and Spirit (I John 5:8).

A Kingdom of Priests

In the first four books of the New Testament, the gospels, the major theme that is spoken of is the kingdom of God. The word spoken by the angel Gabriel to Mary, the virgin who bore the Messiah, was that, "He will be great, and will be called the Son of the Most High; and the Lord God will give Him the throne of His father David; and He will reign over the house of Jacob forever; and His **kingdom** will have no end" (Luke 1:32-33).

[4] "At the time of Christ, many of the Jews were hoping for a political kingdom, a military and geographic realm from which the Jews, under a descendant of David, would rule. They looked back to the time of King David as a golden age in their history, and they longed to return to that time with the promised Messiah as King. They thought a Messiah, referred to as the "Son of Man" in Daniel 7:13- 14, would usher in an eternal kingdom on earth. The Old Testament prophets summarized this hope under the phrase "the day of the Lord," a time in which full restoration would occur (Amos 9:14) and in which the nations would be judged (Amos 1). This was the dream of Jewish

nationalism. The Jewish concept of the kingdom of God explains why the Jews tried to make Jesus king by force during the early part of His ministry; they wanted Him to lead them out from Roman oppression and establish a political kingdom greater than David's."

The Bible clearly teaches us that Jesus Christ was born 'King of the Jews' in the city of Bethlehem. His birth took place in a manger because there was no room for Him in the local inn. Though the rulers of this world did not recognize Him, He came into this earth as a man being born into King David's royal family line (Matt. 2:22).

It was thirty years later in the wilderness of Judea that John the Baptist came preaching, "Repent, for the kingdom of heaven is at hand." John was sent as a voice to prepare the way for the coming King and His kingdom. The last book of the Old Testament, Malachi, ends with the prophecy concerning John the Baptist. "Behold, I am going to send you Elijah the prophet before the coming of the great and terrible day of the Lord" (Malachi 3:2-3). John fulfilled this prophecy (Matthew 17:12) and through the proclamation of the kingdom and water baptism, he prepared the nation of Israel for their King.

> 6 "Another popular understanding of the kingdom of God arose among the Jews during the intertestamental period (approximately 200 B.C. to the New Testament era). This was an adaptation of the prophets' "day of the Lord" theory. The Jews, who went through a series of frightful persecutions during this time, lost hope in an earthly kingdom; they thought God had to destroy the evil present in this age before he could establish His kingdom. They envisioned a new world in which all-evil, demons, sickness, and death would be defeated and eradicated. By dividing history into two periods-evil and good-they set their hope in the age to come.

John, who fulfilled his ministry in the spirit and power of Elijah, told the people to bring forth fruit in keeping with repentance (Luke1:17; Matthew 3:8). John said that "the axe is already laid at the root of the trees; every tree that does not bear good fruit is cut down and thrown into the fire." Just as Elijah brought a separation between those who would serve the God of Abraham, Isaac and Jacob or the idols of religion, politics, pleasure and power, so did John the Baptist. His ministry was one that dealt with the very heart of man, to turn it away from the evil of the present age to the coming King. John, however, was just a preparer of the way for the King who had brought His kingdom to earth.

Once Jesus was baptized by John, empowered with the Holy Spirit and tested in the wilderness, He began to preach and say, "Repent, for the kingdom of heaven is at hand." G.H. Lang in his book 'The Parabolic Teaching of Scriptures' says that:

[6] "Neither John nor Christ said that the kingdom 'is at hand', **in the sense that the KINGDOM OF GLORY** (Outward Kingdom) **could be at once ushered in.** The Greek perfect tense cannot be translated by the English present tense. They said that 'the kingdom has drawn near,' in the sense that *a king is the essence and embodiment of His kingdom, and the kingdom visits a region when he visits it.* This, then, was the inclusive theme of John and Christ. All their teaching was concerned with this kingdom of God and heaven, which is the case with their pictures and parables. Only there were TWO aspects and periods of this kingdom, as foretold by the prophets and was the necessity of the case; an INWARD and an OUTWARD, a *spiritual in the hearts of men, an outward in human affairs*; and the LATTER MUST WAIT FOR THE FORMER." (Emphasis mine)

Jesus came into the world as the 'King of the Jews', was crucified as the 'King of the Jews' (Luke 23:38) and through resurrection from the dead was raised to be seated on the throne of David, just as God had promised. As Peter stood up on the day of Pentecost and preached that first message of the newly formed church, he speaks concerning the resurrection of Christ when he says in Acts 2:29-30 that:

David both died and was buried, and his tomb is with us to this day. And so, because he was a prophet, he knew that GOD HAD SWORN TO HIM WITH AN OATH TO SEAT ONE OF HIS DESCENDANTS UPON HIS THRONE...he looked ahead and spoke of the resurrection of the Christ... (Emphasis mine).

Jesus was raised from the dead, not only as the 'King of the Jews' but also as the 'King of kings and Lord of lords', seated in the very presence of God, ruling from the very throne of God. The book of Revelation pictures Jesus in many ways as the victorious king. Revelation 1:5 says He is, "the faithful witness, the first-born of the dead, and the *ruler of the kings of the earth*". In Revelation 1:18 Jesus says, "I was dead, and behold, I am alive forevermore, and I have the *keys of death and of Hades*." Revelation 5:5 says that Jesus is "the Lion that is from the tribe of Judah, the Root of David and has *overcome*..." Then in Revelation 19:11-16 it pictures the Risen Christ coming to judge the nations.

Jesus has been seated at the very right hand of God not only as the Great High Priest, but also as the ruling King. Jesus is the High Priest after the order of Melchizedek (Hebrews7:17). Melchizedek means: king royal, to reign, to ascend the throne. Jesus is both Priest and King in the same way that David performed both functions to the nation of Israel.

It is not my intention to do an in-depth study of the kingdom of God in this book; however, I want to briefly look at the kingdom as it pertains to the first coming of Christ and what He accomplished. I also want to look at the present reign of Christ from heaven through the church His kingdom of priests.

The First Coming of the King

As we have already seen, prior to the first coming of Christ the Jewish people were looking for a coming Messiah who would give them either political freedom from Rome or destroy the wicked and usher them immediately into the kingdom of God. By taking a look at the Bible we will see what Jesus and His apostles taught concerning the kingdom of God.

Jesus taught that there were two aspects and periods of the kingdom, an INWARD and an OUTWARD. The inward kingdom is spiritual and deals with Christ ruling over individual lives. The outward kingdom is in human affairs and deals with Christ ruling over the nations of the earth. George Ladd sums it up by saying,

[6] "The Kingdom of God is basically the rule of God. It is God's reign, the divine rule in action. God's reign, however, is manifested in several realms, and the Gospels speak of entering into the Kingdom of God both **today** and **tomorrow**. God's reign manifests itself both in the future and in the present and thereby creates both a **future realm** and a **present realm** in which man may experience the blessings of His reign." (Emphasis Mine)

Jesus said the kingdom of God had come in Him and the purpose of the coming of the King was to "destroy the works of Satan." (I John 3:8). As Peter stood up to preach that first message to a group of Gentiles he said,

"You know of Jesus of Nazareth, how God anointed Him with the Holy Spirit and with power, and how He went about doing good, and healing all who were OPPRESSED BY THE DEVIL; for God was with Him." (Acts 10:38; Emphasis Mine**)**

Jesus did more than just announce the kingdom, but He demonstrated the kingdom by healing the sick, casting out demons, and raising the dead, which convinced his listeners that He was the Messiah in whom the kingdom had come. The word kingdom is translated from the Greek word *basileia* found in the New Testament. The word implies an exercise of kingly rule or authority to reign. Jesus demonstrated this kingly rule by delivering men from the bondage and authority of Satan. It was with kingdom power that he commanded unclean spirits to leave people.

[6] "What does the announcement that the Kingdom of God has come near mean? It is this: that God is now acting among men to deliver them from bondage to Satan. It is the announcement that God, in the person of Christ, is...attacking the very kingdom of Satan himself. The exorcism of demons is proof that the Kingdom of God has come among men and is at work among them."

Jesus came to the earth for the sole purpose of destroying the works of the devil. We have seen that in His earthly ministry, He broke the bondage of Satan over many people by healing them, delivering them from evil spirits and even bringing some back to life. However, the plan of the Father was that the Son would die for the sins of the world.

In Hebrews 2:14 we see that it is Jesus' death on the cross, which has 'rendered powerless him who had the power of death, that is, the devil'. In what ways did the cross render powerless the devil? To make it simple, I will say that the devil has no power or right to rule over those who have come under the rule of King Jesus. Those who receive the message of the kingdom of God, have been rescued from the rule of Satan, and have been put under the rule of Jesus Christ (Colossians 1:13).

Satan's power has been bound or rendered powerless over those who have become children of the King and His kingdom. This does not mean evil has been removed from the world, but it does mean that as sons and daughters of God we are no longer subjects of the 'god of this age'. In this age the kingdom of God is offered as a spiritual gift that can be accepted or rejected. If you accept the spiritual rule of the King into your heart, then His power will deliver you from the power of Satan and sin. However, the kingdom of God in its full manifestation has not been ushered in at once but is developing in stages.

The kingdom began with Jesus Christ's birth, death, resurrection, and ascension. Although the world seems unchanged, God's kingdom is here and can be accessed through spiritual rebirth. This kingdom isn't a physical location but a place of spiritual blessings, granted by Christ's actions. Accepting Jesus as Lord means entering His authority and becoming part of His priesthood through the extension of His Spirit.

The Spiritual Kingdom

We have seen that the cross of Christ has broken Satan's power over those who believe. The kingdom of God is not just a future experience but something we can enter now. [6] "The kingdom of God is here; but instead of making changes in the external, political order of things, it is making changes in the spiritual order and in the lives of men and women". According to Hebrews 6:5, it is possible to experience the 'powers of the age to come' in the present. Although we reside in a period marked by evil, these future powers allow us to access the blessings of the kingdom. This creates a conflict that persists until Christ returns to fully establish His kingdom at the end of this era. Currently, entry into the kingdom of God is only attainable through spiritual rebirth by fully surrendering to the power of the cross.

The concept of new birth mentioned in John 3:3-16 refers to accepting Jesus Christ as Lord. It is equated with receiving eternal life and entering the kingdom. The current experience involves the power of the Holy Spirit or the 'powers of the age to come', which is considered the first stage of the kingdom and pertains to the spiritual life of the resurrected Christ within individuals.

Paul says in Romans 14:17 that, "the kingdom of God is not eating and drinking, but righteousness and peace and joy in the Holy Spirit". The spiritual kingdom brings an inward transformation of the heart. When you enter the kingdom of God the Spirit will enter your heart, but it will still be you as far as your natural man is concerned.

The kingdom of God in the heart of man cannot be observed with physical eyes. This does not indicate that the kingdom of God has not entered our hearts; it suggests that the natural human cannot perceive the spiritual realm, which can only be understood through faith. Similar to how one cannot see the wind itself but can observe its effects.

The epicenter of the kingdom is found only in Christ. We often hear about the kingdom of God, and it is encouraging that many understand it. However, separating Christ from the kingdom results in Christianized Humanism. In this age the kingdom is about humility, trust, faithfulness and serving. If you just want to rule over others, then it is a sure sign you are tapping into the kingdom of darkness. Witchcraft's essence lies in using intimidation, manipulation, and domination to control others, not just in spells and incantations.

The kingdom of God is about total identification with Christ so that His Spirit can manifest the power and wisdom of Christ through us. We are not building our own thing but submitting to that which has already been established and cannot be shaken, Christ alone! We can produce nothing of eternal value independent of the power of the Spirit. It is for this reason that we can rest in Him since kingdom fruit is produced by simply being a co-laborer in the grace of God.

Jesus' kingdom has come into this present evil age; in this age, however, it is not an outward political kingdom over and through the nation of Israel but a **spiritual kingdom over the hearts** of those who believe from all nations. Jesus broke Satan's power in His earthly ministry and by His death and resurrection, was raised up to the throne of David as the ruling King-Priest, "far above all rule and authority and power and dominion, and every name that is named, not only in this age, but also in the one to come" (Ephesians 1:20-22).

Jesus is our Great High Priest over the New Temple, which is His church. In Hebrews 12:18-29 the author was showing these Jewish Christians that the kingdom of God is not a physical place, but it is coming underneath the heavenly reign of Christ. To come under the victory of Jesus' resurrection is to enter into the kingdom of God. There is still, however, a future shaking of the created world at the return of Christ when He brings the "Kingdom of Glory" in outward manifestation to rule the nations of the world (Romans 8:18-25; Hebrews 12:27; Matthew 24:29).

Worship and the Kingdom

Worship is about entering into the life of the kingdom of God. It is a process of learning to lay aside our own identity to be clothed in the heavenly garments of our kinsmen-redeemer found in the cross. It is in the fires of worship that idolatry is destroyed, which is anything separating us from His love and blessings so that we are singly focused upon Him; joined to His throne of grace. Idolatry is living in the shadows of duplicity where our affections are divided which brings instability and double mindedness.

John is the author of the gospel named after him, and who also wrote I John, II John, III John and the Revelation. Out of all the authors of the New Testament, John paints a prophetic picture of an epic battle between light and darkness. Our worldview, or how we look at this 'present age,' is important. At the end of John's first epistle, he makes a little statement that we seem to treat like it does not apply to our modern age. John told his spiritual children to *keep themselves from idols* (I John 5:21).

Throughout their history, the children of Israel had a problem with idolatry. However, we don't see the same type of idolatry during the days of Christ as we saw throughout Israel's history. Israel had a history of mixing their faith with the false gods of Baal, making sacrifices on the high places. This was not the problem during the time of Christ.

What was the main rebuke that Jesus gave to the religious leaders of his day? [7] "Israel of Jesus' day was idolatrous because it had worshipped tradition in place of God and His living Word…Israel had substituted reverence for human tradition in the place of love for God." It was for this reason that Jesus told the people that 'they had ears, but they could not hear and eyes, but they could not see'. What happened? When we worship something, we become like the object that we behold.

Israel during the days of Christ worshipped the traditions of men. It was for this reason when the 'Living Word' walked among them they could not hear nor see the kingdom unless they repented and turned away from their idols. The power is not in the idol, but the demonic powers, which draw people to the false worship of idolatry blinding the minds of the worshippers.

An idol is something that keeps us from walking in the fullness of being the worshipful priest our Father is seeking. In this book, I am going to deal with the main idols of Western culture, which are materialism, relativism, and pluralism.

As I have already stated I am a co-pilgrim with you on a journey as a disciple of Christ in this present age in which we all find ourselves living. Modern society presents us with challenges that are unique to our times. The challenges that we face are not new, but the degree to which we are confronting these challenges can seem overwhelming. The kingdom of God is our foundation for worship, and anything not built on that reality will eventually be shaken.

Materialism

In looking at materialism the first thing that will come to most people's minds is the affluence of Western lifestyles. I am going to look at the god of mammon later in Chapter 2, but I want to first look at an ancient heresy which affects us today more than any of us realize.

Gnosticism is a heresy the first century church had to confront. John, in his gospel and epistle confronted the false doctrine that the material world is evil. Gnosticism had many variations, but it basically taught that anything that was material was evil, yet everything of the spirit was good, therefore Jesus could not have come in a human body (I John 4:3). The practical result of this doctrine in the early church and today is that you have to either give in to the unrestrained cravings of our unredeemed bodies since we are powerless to overcome or live as an ascetic monk to brutalize the body, bringing it into subjection.

To the Gnostic, secret knowledge or a subjective mystical insight was the sole key to salvation. Certain Gnostic teachers taught that salvation was not based on what you did, but on the knowledge that you had. If you had the inside knowledge, your conduct did not matter, since salvation was about knowing and not your conduct.

The heresy had many similarities to the teaching that grace is a license to sin and have God overlook your conduct. In applying this teaching to our modern culture, Gnostics become one with materialism since it is futile to resist the lustful cravings of the flesh. It is manifested through many different forms of self-centered addictions, for example sexual sin, chemical dependence or emotional addictions like outbursts of anger, manipulation, intimidation etc. It is what Paul defined as the works of the flesh (Galatians 5:19-21). Gnostics claim they are saved based on what they know, therefore moral character is irrelevant, and they claim our conduct does not affect our relationship with God.

The other extreme position resulting from the 'Gnostic heresy' was a form of ascetic self-denial, which Paul confronted in his epistle to the Colossians. "'Do not touch, do not taste, do not handle,' which all concern things which perish with the using according to the commandments and doctrines of men? These things indeed have an appearance of wisdom in self-imposed religion, false humility, and neglect of the body, but are of no value against the indulgence of the flesh" (Colossians 2:16-23 NKJV).

The practical outcome takes the form of such ascetic behavior as taking a vow of poverty, a vow of celibacy, environmental extremism, ascetic self-denial in eating and dominating others through strict rules etc. In addition, these practices are also simply the work of the flesh manifested through legalism.

The created order is not evil, but it is under a curse and needs redemption (Romans 8:19-20). It is for this reason that we are not to be controlled by the created order, but the inward life of the resurrected Spirit of Christ. The created order includes our unredeemed bodies. The result of materialism is worshiping the creature rather than the creator, which is idolatry (Romans 1:20-32). The son of Man came to redeem, or bring restoration to that which was corrupted because of the curse.

As New Covenant priests we must live in this 'present evil age'. In this age as a people who have been born of the Spirit through the incorruptible seed of God (I Peter 1:23), we still live surrounded by the material world. The Son of God was sent to bring redemption in the midst of a fallen world by taking on our humanity and living as the 'Pattern Son' in this present age.

The book of Hebrews was written to Jewish Christians that were tempted to turn away from total identification with Christ and identify with the law and its system of worship with its religious identification. The design of the book was to clearly detail how the Hebrews could not go back to the Temple, which lay at the center of Hebrew identity. The [8] "readers might well go back to the form of the old covenant and to its worship, but the point remains that, through Jesus, God has rendered this whole system null and void."

The author of Hebrews laid out a clear case to either cling to the old material worship of earthly things or live in the true substance of the heavenly life of the kingdom of God. The types and shadows of the Old Covenant can be an excellent teaching tool, but it must always lead us to our identity in Christ and fellowship with the Father through the Spirit as sons of God.

In the same way, we must turn away from the corruption of this present age and partake of the life of the Spirit. Paul informs us that if we sow to the flesh then we will reap corruption (Gal. 6:8). The word corruption has a meaning of being brought into an inferior or worse condition, but it also means bondage and actual decay. Sowing to the flesh is living life dominated by materialism whether coming under legalism or yielding to self-centered addictions.

The word 'corruption' means decay, and when we sow to the flesh our lives fall apart like a dead carcass in the heat of the day. It does not happen immediately, but the stench of death takes grip on our spiritual lives with the Father. It is a separation from the Spirit of life into ritualism, hedonism, or emotionalism (To get a more detailed study of this subject go to "Building Your Spiritual House" Lesson 10: "A Lifestyle of Repentance").

Western thought looks at spirituality as being detached from this world, but we have been called in the same way that Christ came into this creation to heal, restore, and deliver by the power of the Spirit. We are not supposed to have a division between what we call secular and spiritual areas of our lives. [9] "As trustees and stewards of God's world, human beings were to live within it and use it in accord with divine directives. Again, in Paul's familiar Hebraic idiom, 'Whatever you do, work at it with all your heart, as working for the Lord, not for men'" (Col. 3:23).

We are called to holistic worship, which includes our bodies, hearts, speech, conduct, relationships, work, finances; our whole lives bringing glory to God. Worship includes the material world; however, it is the created world being subject to the redeeming work of the Triune God. A priest is one who displays the very nature of redemption in and through our whole lives. We are called up into His priesthood not to leave this present age, but we are called to be free from the corruption of this present age while at the same time bringing restoration to others.

Mt. Zion cannot be entered through the material realm but only entered through the Spirit. The fullness of the kingdom brought at the return of Christ will be the power and glory of the kingdom totally transforming the material world. The first thing to be transformed is going to be our bodies bringing us into the fullness of our salvation and bringing the fullness of Christ's rule to the nations. Until then we are seated in heavenly places with Him ruling in His authority. It is from this position of resting in the presence of the Father that we exercise spiritual warfare, overcoming the powers of darkness through priestly prayer.

Relativism

Relativism could be defined as situational ethics. To say, for example, "It may be wrong for you, but it is right for me in this context." I concur that context will change our understanding of a situation, but it should never change our ethics. Have you ever had something happen in a certain context which was extremely funny? Then you try and retell the story outside of that context and it is not funny any longer? How about language and context? I use this analogy often to make a point. 'Les Tabernacles' does not mean anything to English speakers, but if you use the word in Quebec,

Canada it is like saying the "F..." word in English. If you want to define relativism as contextual, I will agree with you.

Let's look at the gospel regarding the first century disciples. The Jewish believers could not imagine the gospel going outside of a Jewish context. It took a spiritual encounter for Peter to share the gospel outside of a Jewish context (Acts 10). Eternal truth never changes, but the gospel can become incarnated in varying context. Truth never changes, but application can vary depending on the context. The issue with relativism is moral relativism, where truth changes based on context. Instead of truth shaping us, we alter it to suit our needs. This results in lawlessness.

We are no longer under the legal requirements of the Civil and Ceremonial Law of Moses; however, the Moral Law is the eternal nature of God. Antinomianism was a heresy during the first century church. The word comes from two Greek words: *anti* means against and *nomos* means law. We must make a distinction between Civil Authority as described in Romans 13 and spiritual authority administered by the church.

The church is subject to civil laws and is commanded to pray for those governments that rule by civil law. The place of the Mosaic Law was one of the greatest disputes in the early church. The issue of circumcision and the keeping of the Ceremonial Law was a major debate. Circumcision was given to Abraham and the children of Israel as a sign that they were covenant children of God. At the age of eight days all male Israelites had their foreskin cut.

Certain Jewish Christians began to teach that for a Gentile or non-Jew to be accepted by God as covenant partner with Him then they too must be circumcised and obey the Ceremonial Law. Paul the apostle who was born a Jew (Philippians 3:4-6) refuted this false teaching. He taught that both Jew and Gentile are saved on the basis of faith in the free gift of Christ.

In Colossians 2:11 Paul says that it is not the circumcision in the flesh that matters, but the circumcision of the heart. It is faith in Christ, which places us into the family of God, not the keeping of the Law. However, this does not give us the right to worship false gods, covet, kill or even allow immoral thoughts to captivate our hearts. Jesus did not come to destroy the law, but to fulfill it and He did.

I will use an analogy from nature to try to help us understand the fulfillment of the Law. In central Texas we have a lot of stock ponds and if you put big mouth bass in your stock ponds, they will eat up all the smaller fish. The main covenants in the Bible are the Abrahamic, Mosaic and Davidic, which were all fulfilled or consumed by Christ. When you catch a bass, you see only the bass, but all those other fish are a part of the bass. In the same way when we look at Christ, all of the other covenants are in Him, but our focus is to be completely upon the blood covenant and resurrected Son of God.

As New Covenant priest's we are to have the Moral Law written upon on our hearts by the Spirit of God (Hebrews 8:7-13). If we are in fellowship with God worshipping Him, then we cannot be living in continued acts of sin which the apostle John called living in darkness (I John 1:6). We are not to be religious legalists who live by the letter, but there is a standard of holiness revealing the character of God in the Moral Law.

God's holy character has not passed away! Look at the book of Revelation 21:8, which says those who practice wickedness, are not allowed into the kingdom. Read the writings of Jesus and all of His apostles and you will see that those who practice lawlessness and reject holiness will be judged in this life and the life to come.

Pluralism

In looking at pluralism, there is a clear difference in the way of the kingdom and how the world views this subject. In the world, pluralism is seen as taking the many and making them into one. Babylon, which is symbolic of the fullness of the nations in rebellion towards God, sees diversity as merging the world religious systems, political systems and economic systems into one system.

Babylon highly esteems pluralism, as long as there is a willingness to conform to the image. We see this especially in the image that Nebuchadnezzar set up for all to worship. Anyone who refuses to submit to the conformed pattern is bullied and forced into submission.

Babylonian pluralism teaches that all religions lead to the same place, which we could call syncretism. Israel had a long history with syncretism, and it was the very source of God's judgments upon the nation when they mixed their faith with the customs of the nations.

Paul in I Corinthians 10 uses Israel as an example not to follow regarding living a life dedicated to worship. In the wilderness, while Moses was receiving the law and instructions about worship, the children of Israel were making an idolatrous golden calf similar to the Egyptian gods (Exodus 32). Israel was God's covenant people set apart to serve God so that they would bear His likeness in the midst of the nations. It was the Father's intent to have a people set apart by covenant so that He could dwell with them, but they refused to stay faithful.

Israel's history is riddled with mixing among the nations and being corrupted from within. When you embrace syncretism, the result is defilement. The Old Testament is filled with prophetic pleas for the people to return to covenant faithfulness as an unfaithful bride returning to the purity of marriage.

The world does not understand true freedom or the diversity of true unity since it is only the Spirit of God, which can produce unity. Kingdom living is the exact opposite of worldly conformity. In the kingdom of God out of the one seed of Christ comes diversity. In the kingdom, we are transformed to be ourselves so that our lives display the glory of God. True worship brings transformation to be ourselves in the presence of God and function in our purpose as a priest in the kingdom.

Israel came from one father yet had the diversity of 12 unique tribes who were to rule their portion, or inheritance. In the same way the High Priestly garments had the 12 stones of each tribe placed within the breastplate that he wore representing the unity, yet diversity of the kingdom.

We each have a common foundation, but we also each have an individual part to fulfill, which makes us unique in God's mighty plan. The Holy Spirit empowers us to be like Christ and to be ourselves. This is called the manifold wisdom of God (Ephesians 3:10). Just as Joseph had a coat of many colors, so God has woven a beautiful tapestry together called the body of Christ. The body is made up of many individual colors masterfully woven together through the wisdom of God to display the likeness of Christ.

The Threshing Floor

The very foundation of worship is a place of sifting where the Spirit is creating a heart, which will be a habitation for His presence. True worship is built upon the very foundation of Christ. Since the fall of man, the Spirit has been moving history to bring us to the final consummation, which is the summing up of all things in Christ (Ephesians 1:10).

In our modern outlook of history, we fail to see the two-sided coin of salvation and judgment. The cross is our foundation, yet it is a place of salvation: restoration, reconciliation, mercy, while at the same time a place of judgment: separation, sifting, holiness produced by the consuming fire of the Spirit. The book of Revelation is an unfolding of God's judgments in history meant to turn humanity back to Christ.

The Hebrew word *mishpat,* which is translated into the English word judgment, can be defined as a *sifting out.* [10] "Thus, judgment is not only a final, curtain-dropping event but also a lengthy process with God as an active investigator testing people's hearts, giving the wicked a chance to repent." Peter tells us that it is not God's heart that any would perish, but He desires all to come to the full understanding of the truth (II Peter 3:9).

Worship on the threshing floor is the great equalizer. It is a place of total surrender where the arrogant soul is humbled and the downtrodden is lifted up. Hannah, the mother of Samuel, who was a great transitional figure in the Old Testament preparing the way for the king-priest ministry of David, had a similar word as Mary the mother of Jesus.

[11] "Mary celebrated *mishpat* as an upside-down reversal of the current state of affairs. 'He has brought down rulers from their thrones but has lifted up the humble' (Luke 1:52)." The great equalizer is Christ where "there is neither Jew nor Greek, there is neither slave nor free man, there is neither male nor female, for you are all one in Christ Jesus" (Galatians 3:28).

The threshing floor is a place of crushing and separation where all things are laid open and naked before the Lord of the harvest. The threshing floor was also symbolic of the relationship between the bride and the bridegroom. It is not insignificant that Ruth came to Boaz at the 'threshing floor' (Ruth 3:6-14). Boaz represents Christ (our kinsman-redeemer) and Ruth, the bride of Christ. At the center of the threshing floor, one finds two large flat stones, one resting on the top of the other. They were fitted and joined together. The top stone was known as the female and the bottom stone the male, the grinding of grain was a depiction of the act of marriage (Job 31:10).

In looking at worship, the threshing floor was used to

separate grain from the chaff at harvest time. Judgment is actually redemptive in the sense that the Spirit of God is attempting to remove from our lives that which is not beneficial to us so that we can be totally joined to the Lord and one with Him. Threshing floors were normally located on hilltops because of the need for wind in the process of winnowing, where the lighter chaff would blow to one side while the grain would fall back onto the floor. It is a place where we are separated completely unto God or as the old-time preachers used to call it "sanctification". If we want to have consistent fellowship with the Father, then we must be a people of holiness.

Worship is a place of sifting while at the same time it is a place of communion and union. Hebrews says that the kingdom we are receiving is unshakable because God is our consuming fire who removes everything in us that can be shaken in order that we remain faithful to our union with Christ. It is out of the place of total surrender that we are to offer to God lives of service (Hebrews 12:26-29). It is in this place that the Father takes pleasure in prospering us for our enjoyment and His.

The worship centers of Israel, like David's tabernacle and Solomon's temple, were laid on the foundation of the threshing floor and it is the place that the priesthood ministered before the Lord (I Chronicles 21:18-30). The Father is bringing forth a kingdom of priests. It is important for us to always remember that we are not alone but are born into the family. It is supposed to be a family that works together in unity and harmony. We are purchased with the same blood, washed in the same water, and filled with the same Spirit (I John 5:5-8). We have overcome the world by the power of the same covenant, and we must stand together.

Our unity is found in our one identity. Psalm 133 focuses upon the High Priest as the focal point of the Hebrew nation's identity and the source of their unity. Jesus in John chapter 17 as our High Priest prayed that we would be a unified priesthood. We cannot produce unity, but by having 'our identity' in the one who is our 'all in all,' we remain faithful to the foundation where we are all equally one in Christ.

Worship is about keeping Christ as our center and refusing to yield to any form of idolatry. The three Hebrew young men refused the idolatrous worship of Babylon, and the fire only destroyed the cords of the enemy (Daniel 3:25-27). Fire is a place where we are tested and surrender. It is a place where overcoming faith is manifested. It is fire which tests our faith, and it is faith that gives us victory. It also means that we are faithful to our purpose, refusing to be defiled by the corruption of this age. The Father is looking for a faithful priesthood that will be true to His purpose.

The last book before Jesus first coming is the book of Malachi. In the book, he deals with the priesthood and in a very practical way. Worship affects all areas of our lives and as I have already said, our worship is to be holistic. We cannot live compartmentalized lives where we allow God only into certain areas of our lives. Compartmentalization is not worship, but idolatrized hypocrisy.

In the book of I Samuel 2:31-35, God was rebuking Eli the High Priest for his unfaithful sons who polluted the priesthood. They abused their place of authority, were sexually immoral, greedy and therefore God brought judgment upon them for their excesses. God expects us to be faithful priests over the calling of God on our lives, our relationships, and our finances. In all areas of our lives, He desires us to be faithful.

It is the fire of God, which produces a pure priesthood. The prophet said, "the day is coming like a furnace; and all the arrogant and every evildoer will be chaff; and the day that is coming will set them ablaze,' says the Lord of hosts, 'so that it will leave them neither root nor branch.'" (Malachi 4:1) We can only offer up pure worship on the threshing floor with clean hands and a pure heart free from idolatry. (Psalm 24: 3-5)

The Foundation of Sound Doctrine

The end of the age is said by Jesus to be a time of harvest when the winds of separation are blowing on the threshing floor of the nations. It is for this reason that grounding is needed since confusion will abound. People tend to look at sound doctrine as the shallow teaching of scripture; however, it is the pillars of sound doctrine that go deep into the ground, keeping our lives securely centered in Christ during troubled times.

Jesus rebuked the Pharisees for focusing on doctrine and traditions to the exclusion of worshipping God. He told them that they search the scriptures thinking that the Bible was an end to itself (John 5:39). However, He explained to them that the purpose of the scriptures, or word of God, is to reveal the Father so that we may have fellowship. The scriptures are to lead us to a relationship with Christ and worship of the Father; the Bible is not an end to itself, which would be making the Bible an idol.

Salvation involves deliverance and transformation through a relationship with Christ. Sound doctrine is crucial, as Paul emphasized to Titus (Titus 2:1), because it fosters healthy living and holistic worship. Mere knowledge can lead to spiritual pride (I Corinthians 8:1) without application. True worship integrates truth into every aspect of life without compartmentalization.

Paul instructed us that the "goal of our instruction is love from a pure heart and a pure heart and a clear conscience and a sincere faith" (I Timothy 1:5 Emphasis Mine). You see it is only faith that will please God, not abiding by rules and regulations, or just agreeing with certain facts. Romans 10:17 says "faith comes from hearing, and hearing by the word of Christ or the word concerning Christ". So as we hear the word of God, we want to become "obedient from the heart to the form or 'pattern' of teaching that has been committed to us" (Romans 6:17).

Love must also be one of our main goals as we learn the word of God. In I Corinthians 13 we are told that if we know all mysteries and all knowledge...but have not love, we are nothing. It is important to try and avoid the pitfall of legalism, which can happen when we make learning sound doctrine an end in itself. In looking at being a faithful priesthood, it is important that we grow in grace and love, not just knowledge.

As a priest, we must have a clear conscience. Hebrews 9:14 says that our conscience is cleansed by the blood of Christ, not based on our works, but the revelation of the Spirit by the word of God. The word of God should produce in us a clear awareness of ourselves in our relationship to our Father, so that we can fulfill His purposes in this life. If our conscience is not clear, then it will hinder our relationship with Him and spoil our testimony before the world. It should be our desire to have the same testimony as Paul the apostle had when he said, "I thank God, whom I serve with a clear conscience" (II Timothy 1:3).

The New Testament priesthood is about praying the prayer of Christ. It is learning to pray with our whole lives; that the kingdom of God comes into the earth with practical application. Wisdom is the ability to apply truth so that our lives work the way that they were created to work. We have been created in Christ to do good works, or you might say serve as priests (Ephesians 2:10).

In Zechariah, where Joshua the priest was clothed with clean and pure garments, there is a stone with seven eyes (Zechariah 3:9). In this text, the number seven speaks of the Holy Spirit, and the stone speaks of Christ our foundation. Isaiah 11:2, in speaking about Christ he lists the sevenfold anointing. The anointing oil of the Spirit is upon our very foundation, and it is on this very foundation that the holy priesthood is brought forth (I Peter 2:5-9). The priesthood is to proclaim through our holistic worship the light of His nature in the midst of darkness.

Christ, the wisdom of God, is our foundation, and the end of the age is going to bring shaking; however, if we will tap into the wisdom of the Spirit we will build on the kingdom foundation. Wisdom is not limited to knowledge but taps into the very heart of God to bring solutions and restoration. In this book, we are going to focus on the wisdom of God, developing a relationship with God, and walking in this world as light.

Chapter 2

THE TALE OF TWO CITIES

"The waters which you saw where the harlot sits are peoples and
multitudes and nations and tongues."
~Revelation 17:15~

Have you ever been to a powerful city like New York,
London, Hong Kong, or Paris? Even if you have never been to one
of these cities you have been influenced by their power in some form.
Out of these powerful cities emanate great financial centers that
affect world markets, media that affects culture and even apparel that
affects the way we each dress and look. We are impacted and
connected around the world by these major populations of people
and power.

In the Bible, we see two cities battling for power to influence
mankind. The 'spirit of Babylon', which represents the futile attempts
of man inspired by Satan to make God in His image and the 'city of
God,' or the church whose builder and maker is God. One City
descends from above; the other city is built from the earth trying to
ascend to the heights of heaven. These two cities represent two
systems. One system is the kingdom of God empowered by the
Holy Spirit, and the other system is the world, empowered by the
principalities and powers of darkness.

These two systems are also portrayed as two women.
Women represent intimacy, spiritual union, and covenant. The book
of Proverbs contrasts these two women. One is a virtuous woman
and the other is an insolent rebellious harlot. They are both
presented as crying out for our attention. The harlot tries to gain our
attention by appealing to our fleshly desires and arrogant motives of
power. At the same time, the virtuous woman is gently persuading us
to walk in the fear of the Lord. The harlot finds its ultimate
fulfillment in the Babylon referred to in Revelation 14, 17 and 18.

The other is the virtuous woman, the bride of Christ, finding its ultimate fulfillment in Revelation 19 at the marriage supper of the Lamb.

Biblical interpretation is a very controversial subject, and men have even fought many battles in the past and presently over the subject. I'm a stickler when it comes to foundational doctrine, but I refuse to be dogmatic when it comes to more speculative areas of scripture like the book of Revelation. I present some general ideas of interpretation concerning the book of Revelation, but solid scholars from whom I have learned a tremendous amount take alternative views.

All you must do is look in your town to see the number of denominations who have separated many times over minor issues. I refuse to separate over differing views of biblical interpretation when it is not an area that affects our eternal salvation. The book of Revelation can be complex, speculative and in the hands of some a dangerous writing. I write this material with a bit of trepidation in my heart, hoping that you will give me the liberty to explore and push the boundaries of conventional understanding to present a viewpoint which I hope will benefit the modern reader.

Western thinkers have been greatly influenced by Greco-Roman, Renaissance and Enlightenment thinking; therefore, we like to have things put into logical, sequential order. We do not like things with ragged edges or something that seem to be out of order; that is why when you look at most of the prophecy teachers, they have well-defined charts with everything in its proper place. I glean a tremendous amount from many of these teachers, but prophecy is like life, and we all know that life does not happen nice and tidy.

Life gets messy! We read history and we look to see what happened on a specific date. What we often fail to see is what happened before and after that date. Life is fluid and does not happen in an orderly fashion, so it is with prophecy. [1] "Most prophecy is written in poetry rather than prose and so partakes of a certain measure of ambiguity with its numerous figures of speech."

Let's look at the life of Christ, who I can confidently say has been the most transformative man that has ever been born. We see that He was born, and the heavens declared His arrival, but He did not get public recognition until He reached the age of thirty when He began performing miracles. His ministry time on earth was short, and then after He rose from the dead, He appeared to many for the next 40 days before His final ascension to the Father.   Christ's first coming was not just one event, but a series of events over a period of time and actually the two time periods of the Old and New covenant overlapped one another for a season of time. Heaven invaded the earth, and you could not take a knife out and make a clean cut. It was not like a movie where you can clean up the parts you do not understand but was the 'Giver of Life' invading history, which is more complex and organic. How much more will His final return be a fluid series of events, putting His enemies under His feet as a final climatic event on the Mount of Olives in Jerusalem?

The Pharisees thought they had it all figured out, but many of them missed the Messiah for whom they were looking. We need humility of heart like Anna and Simeon in the Temple (Luke 2:25-38) at the time of Jesus' dedication, to see with the eyes of our heart, what others may not recognize. Christ's first coming was not packaged the way most scholars thought He should come. Even those who witnessed the fulfillment did not always comprehend what was taking place. I am sure His return will similarly have some turns in the road we do not expect, but if we are walking with 'The Resurrection' we will understand the way.

Westerners don't like to live with mystery, but like everything scientifically figured out and in its proper order. Life has a bit of mystery to it, and prophecy is the same way. In looking at our Hebraic roots, we find a culture, which has historically had a respect for not having all the answers and accepting a certain amount of mystery. [1] "Usually the prophets, as they looked into the future, spoke of coming events without attempting to give the temporal sequence of the several stages of the accomplishment of God's purpose. Not only is the distant future viewed as a single although complex event, but the immediate future are described as though they constituted a single act of God."

The 'day of the Lord' was a major prophetic theme of the prophets, which was to be a time when God would invade the present age and bring history to its final climax.   It is to be a time of judgment for the wicked, and salvation for the believer. It is when the God of history brings this present age to a close and thrusts us into the age to come. However, it does not seem to be just one decisive act, but a period of time, or a transitional time period. The proverbial icing on the cake will be the return of Christ, or more popularly termed His second coming to this earth, which will trigger the complete transformation to which we are all moving towards.

One thing we see in the book of Revelation is a complex series of events where mankind loses control while all things that can be shaken are shaken. We have seven seals, seven trumpets and seven bowls which seem to be different but more intense views of the same act. However, the one thread that we need to focus upon is not shaking, but the unshakable One; the Lamb whom we must humbly worship. In the midst of fluid change and difficulties, He remains the same; therefore, we must keep our undivided attention on Him, who is the only one who is worthy of opening the seals.

I have read multiple commentaries on the book of Revelation from varying authors using different methods of interpretation. I have gleaned tremendous insight from each one of these differing views. I agree with aspects of each view. However, with much that I have read, I am almost always left with no applicable truth other than the first three chapters. One of the goals of my writing is to apply the truth, so again I ask that you give me the liberty to address the place where we live day-to-day.

In applying Babylon to our modern culture, I am going to use a Jewish method of interpretation called Midrash. [3] "To the ancient Jewish mind, prophecy was pattern which is recapitulated; a prophecy having multiple fulfillments. And each fulfillment, each cycle, teaches something about the ultimate fulfillment." Multiple authors see the Passover pattern in the book of Revelation, and I agree that it is a clear pattern in the book. However, in Revelation 14, 17 and 18 we also see the Babylonian pattern portrayed in the book of Revelation.

Let's go to the book of Genesis chapter 11 and look at the origin of the ancient city of Babylon, which goes back to the tower of Babel when men tried to build a tower reaching to heaven. After the flood, Nimrod assembled people together to build a system opposition to God and a tower where they would escape God's wrath. It was to be a utopian society where men could rule as god and bring peace on earth.

The Babylonians understood "Babel" which the tower was named to mean '*the gate of the god*,' or you might say a pathway to God. The Hebrews understood "Babel" to mean 'mixed up, confused' or you could say a '*confused mixture*'. The city of Babel became a place where men could unite in pursuit of their own lustful desires and unadulterated power. Though God scattered the people and broke their communication, Babylon eventually became one of the first global cities dominating the ancient world.

> [4] "The power of the city of Babylon was linked to its idolatry…Human rebellion is expressed through its worship, which is also is built into its systems of security and protection. God is no longer the hiding place and refuge of humanity, but men seek to construct their own refuge, with idolatry at its heart, in a deliberate and persistent attempt to avoid doing the will of God. "

In an antithesis to the idolatrized confusion of worship at Babel, God calls the father of faith Abraham. Abraham along with his family members were all idolaters. They followed the polytheistic (worshipers of multiple idol gods) religious practices established and spread throughout the nations when God confused and scattered the people at Babel.

Acts 7:2 describes Abrahams encounter. "The God of glory appeared to our father Abraham when he was in Mesopotamia before he lived in Haran, and said to him, 'DEPART FROM YOUR COUNTRY AND YOUR RELATIVES, AND COME INTO THE LAND THAT I WILL SHOW YOU'" (emphasis mine). [4]"Having heard the voice of God, Abraham's life and worship are thus transformed…In this way the covenant formed with Abraham, and his believing response to it, act as implicit and abiding criticisms of the nations' worship, typified in Babel. For the rest of the patriarchal narratives Abraham…**related to God by covenant and promise**, rather than by **location** or **ritual**."

Abraham was impacted by the supernatural power from above, and as a result, he was inspired by faith in the covenant promise to look for "the city which has foundations, whose architect and builder is God" (Heb. 11:10). Abraham lived his days by faith as an alien and a foreigner in the land he was promised. However, due to his faith in the unseen city, we can now partake of the promise.

All men and women of faith have been those who refuse to settle for anything less than pursuing the full purpose of God which will ultimately be brought to consummation during the 'day of the Lord'. When all is said and done, what is truly going to matter is did we build our lives on the only foundation that cannot be shaken, Christ Himself who is the epicenter of the kingdom?

In the book of Genesis, we see a prophetic pattern that finds its way into the book of Revelation. Babylon is about conformity to the collective will. It is the essence of materialism, relativism and pluralism where self is the center. The tower was built out of man-made brick, which is a picture of man joining their efforts together under the curse.

The best Babylon can produce is man-made, or the fullness of man, which is the full maturity of wickedness, or man's full rebellion against God, symbolized by the number 666 (A tremendous amount of debate surrounds what Revelation 13:7 describes as 'the mark', 'the name of the beast or the number of his name'. I am not going to enter the speculation of the exact details concerning what the 'mark of the beast' has been or will be depending on your interpretive approach).

It is interesting to look at Peter's words when speaking about Christ's coming and likening it to the days of Noah. He used the term 'day of the Lord' comparing it to Noah's day when by water the fullness of man's wickedness was judged and removed from the earth so that a righteous seed would remain. The rainbow is a demonstration that water will never be used again, but a judgment of fire is being kindled to thoroughly cleanse the threshing floor and cleanse the earth of wickedness. (II Pt 3:3-18)

> [5] "Jesus said the days prior to His return would be as the days of Noah…God did not give Noah a predetermined date specifying when the flood would come. The Lord gave Noah two things: a task, which was to build the ark, and time to get the job done."

In like manner we have been commissioned to build the *ekklesia*, which is the church and preaching the gospel. Abraham is the prototype of a kingdom builder who walks by faith with a life centered on Christ the foundation. The kingdom is about individuality built together displaying diversity. Paul says that we are individual living stones willingly built together to form a habitation of God's Spirit (Eph. 1:22). Our collective unity is found in the Spirit of God anointing us individually, where we willingly lay down our lives to serve God and one another. It is unity found in our diversity established on one foundation.

Amid the religious confusion of our day, the original promise given to the father of our faith is a source of true worship with which we can totally identify. It is in the book of Galatians where we can understand the blessing that we are to inherit by faith through Abraham. The book of Galatians says that through Abraham "ALL THE NATIONS SHALL BE BLESSED…in order that **in Christ Jesus** the blessing of Abraham might come to the Gentiles (nations), so that we might **receive the promise of the Spirit** through faith." (Gal. 3:8,14).

The only place in the New Testament where the term 'blessing of Abraham' is mentioned is here in Galatians 3:14. The Amplified Translation says it like this, "To the end that through [their receiving] Christ Jesus, the blessing [promised] to Abraham might come upon the Gentiles, so that we through faith might [all] receive [the realization of] the promise of the [Holy] Spirit." It does not promise us the security of material wealth nor a physical land, but that we would be receivers of the Spirit, inheriting the "city of God" descending down from above. It is a focus upon Christ Himself and the blessing of the Spirit poured out through His resurrection, ascension and dominion at the right hand of the Father.

I am not saying that God is not going to bless us with money or land, but I am saying the blessing of Abraham is the promise of the Spirit through Christ the final seed of Abraham (Galatians 3:16). At the same time, if we are walking with God, we understand that we are simply stewards of all we have, and we must always be willing to give up everything but Him.

Moses said it was the Spirit of God that separated the descendants of Abraham from the nations of the earth (Exodus 33:16). It does not take long to live in this world to realize that the unbeliever can have possessions and money. It is not material possessions that separate the believer from the world, but the Spirit of life, and we must be willing to do whatever it takes to keep fresh oil in our lamps so that we can be the light which Christ has called us to be (Matthew 25:4).

God Takes Pleasure in Our Prosperity

Success and prosperity are terms that Westerners have heard all of their life. As Christians, we need to be able to live in our culture yet fulfill the will of God. Worship is about living holistic lives where our whole lives give glory to God therefore holistic prosperity brings wholeness.

The book of Deuteronomy 8:18 states that God has given His children the power to get wealth. It is amazing to look at history as the Jewish people have been some of the most despised, rejected, persecuted, and wealthy people since their conception.

I want to give you my definition of what I call biblical success. **Success is completing and fulfilling the will of God for your life.** It is not about possessing wealth, properties, vehicles, or material desires. It involves understanding an individual's purpose and fulfilling it in a practical manner.

The Greek word used for prosper is *euodo* and its meaning is *"to help on one's way or journey."* The problem is that many have interpreted the Bible through their cultural preference. We can't make the Bible fit our lifestyle, but we must let the Bible define our lifestyle. True biblical prosperity is not focused upon money, but upon fulfilling the purpose of God.

God desires us to prosper, yet biblical prosperity can be taught on any continent and in any nation on the face of the earth. I define prosperity as **"having enough to accomplish the will of God"**. You need prosperity to have success on your journey. Yes, this means you will need money, but prosperity is more than money. Prosperity includes everything you will need to help you fulfill the purpose of God for your life and have a successful journey while in this body.

I like what Solomon wrote when he said that the blessing of the Lord gives us all that we need and more but adds no sorrow to it (Proverbs 10:22). Wealth that is not Christ-centered has the overwhelming potential to destroy us. Success and prosperity that is Christ-centered by following the will of God will be a blessing to our lives and the lives of others. However, if we allow wealth to become our focus, or simply succeeding for ambitions sake we will discover an overwhelming corruption that will be demonstrated with sorrow. Oh, the numbers of people who have spent years climbing the proverbial corporate ladder or ministerial ladder realize when they got to the top they were by themselves, and not fulfilled, but sorrowful.

The Father wants to bless the works of our hands and takes pleasure in doing so (Psalms 90:17). The blessing of God is when our lives are empowered to fulfill His purpose, but we have to be on the journey of His pilgrimage to receive all that He wants us to possess.

The blessing of Abraham is that we can be worshipers of the

Living God by His Sprit, and that our worship is not bound to a certain geographical location or religious ritual. It seems that this is the central message that John was trying to relate to us in the Revelation: a Christ centered message.

John did not promise us that we would have earthly security, wealth or political power, but that through being worshippers of the Living God by total identification with Christ we would be those who overcome the world by faith. It is an understanding that no matter what situation in life we find ourselves that our lives will bring glory to God because we are living a life totally dedicated to Him.

LIGHT IN THE MIDST OF BABYLON

The gospel is intended to affect all aspects of our life and even society. It is the responsibility of each member of the body of Christ to use their gifts wherever the Lord places them. It is the breaking down of false ideas that separate the clergy from the laity, the sacred from the secular.

If you have a teaching gift, it does not necessarily mean you are to serve in a traditional church way, but you may teach in a school or university. You could use your gift to be a motivational teacher to business leaders. We are called to impact this world, and we are the church no matter where we have been called to serve. Education is a kingdom that has been taken over with Babylonian thinking, and you may be called to be a Daniel in the midst of Babylon.

A missional movement applies the gospel to all spheres of life. It is nothing new, but large segments of the body of Christ are finally awakening to the fact of our being a kingdom of priests. It is not the Father's desire to leave anyone in the dark and they cannot see unless He has a light in the dark place. We are a fragrance of the Living God and we are to carry His scent into the entire world. (II Corinthians 2:14)

[6] "Our job as Christians is not to take over the various communities in our world; it is however, to penetrate them, to be present, to provide God's alternative to evil, to demonstrate Christ's relevance there, to be as good a representative as possible for Him and His church."

It is important that we are not afraid to go where darkness

dwells. If we are walking in the light, then we should always believe that darkness is being pushed back by the presence of our lives. Jesus also used the analogy of our lives being like salt, which is supposed to bring preservation to ungodly influences surrounding us. It was God's hand that put Esther, Joseph and Daniel in the king's presence. They did not run and hide from ungodly kings, but at the proper time spoke truth to power with the humility of wisdom.

ALL ROADS LEAD TO ROME

  Paul fittingly termed Christ's first coming as the **'fullness of times.'** His arrival was timed perfectly! Christ stepped into time during the rule of the Roman Empire. This was during a period when there was basically a one-world system connecting different peoples together and an adequate road system by which they could easily travel.
  Rome had extensive trade routes established on land and sea. The Roman roads are one lasting legacy of Roman domination, and many are still in use today. The roads were used for moving military much in the same way the U.S. and Germany originally built its modern highway system to move troops and weapons. However, the greatest benefit of a large network of roads was the transport of goods.
  Rome started as a city-state and eventually became a vast empire. Rome was culturally and economically inter-connected. In addition, they extended citizenship far beyond the people of Italy to Greeks and Gauls, Spaniards and Syrians, Jews and Arabs, North Africans and Egyptians. The Roman Empire also became the channel through which the cultures and religions of many peoples were combined. David Pawson says,

[7] "The 'preterist' (refer to Appendix A to understand the term preterist) school of interpretation applies Babylon' to the metropolis of Rome. There is some ground for doing so, not least because this was probably the way original readers of Revelation would take it. One of Peter's letters, written for a very similar purpose (to prepare saints for suffering), may already have made this coded link (I Peter 5:13). And the reference to 'seven hills' would probably clinch it (Rev. 17:9, though not that the 'hills' represent kings). Rome's decadent

character would also fit the description in Revelation. Her seductive attraction of goods and finance in return for favors rendered and her domination of petty kings fit the picture well. Yet it is doubtful if this is the total fulfillment. **Rome was certainly a Babylon. But only a fore shadowing of the Babylon, which dominates the end of history.**" (Emphasis mine)

GLOBALIZATION

In the same way that the first coming of Christ was termed the "fullness of times", His return will be at the right time of history. I started this chapter with a verse from Revelation 17, and in it we are given a view of the nations of the earth just before the return of Christ and the end of the age. We are told that the "waters which you saw where the harlot sits, are peoples and multitudes and nations and tongues." It is here where we see that the prostitute system of Babylon is going to connect peoples and multitudes and nations and tongues together into one system under her seducing power at the end of the age.

Babylon is symbolic of a system which is unstable, constantly moving, and volatile, which water represents. In the same way that Jesus used 'birth pangs' (Matthew 24:8) to describe the growing intensity of the end of the age in like manner the waters represent the nations in uproar (Psalms 2:1) and disarray at the end of the age. As we reach the final climax of this present age, we will see great volatility and instability. At the same time, the bride of Christ will be established on an unshakable kingdom with no end (Daniel7:13- 14). How the kingdom is to be manifested in this age before Christ return to the earth is of great debate. However, there is no debate about our lives being saved, delivered and eternally secure in Christ who is the epicenter of the unshakable kingdom of God.

Today we are not connected by roads, but something more instant and available the electronic communication of our new age. Global capital does not move by physical assets and hands anymore. At the mere touch of a button, trillions of dollars can be moved and commercial transactions are performed.

I can turn on my TV in central Texas and watch China's Central Television Network. You can sit outside of a café in Istanbul, Turkey, and with wireless internet perform business transactions with a businessman in Buenos Aires, Argentina. Our inter-connectedness is actually mind boggling if you sit back sometime and think about it. The Bible shows us a picture of a powerful global enterprise that will connect the peoples of the earth together at the end of the age.

Globalism is a philosophy that emphasizes the current trend toward international organizations and institutions. Globalization is the integration of nation-states, through increasing contact, communication, and trade, to create an integrated economy and governing oversight for all humanity.

> [8] "A leading globalization theorist, Robertson shows how cultures and societies - along with their members and participants - are being squeezed together and driven towards increased mutual interaction. He describes this as 'the compression of the world'. As shared forces and exchanges powerfully structure our lives so the world is becoming one place and one system."

God said of the original Babel that "they are one people, and they all have the same language…now nothing which they purpose to do will be impossible for them." (Gen 11:6) Just as the interconnectedness of Rome provided ample means for the spread of the gospel during the first century, today's global communication will benefit the spreading of the gospel of the kingdom to all nations.

We are seeing this impact as nations shut off to traditional missionaries are being affected by such avenues as Facebook and Twitter with new sorts of communication technology surely to be developed in the future. In the same way that Paul took advantage of his situation we need to use every avenue to spread the gospel.

BABYLONIAN COVETOUSNESS

It is not hard to notice that contemporary culture is driven by the desire to possess and from where does this drive originate? It is important to look at this issue because it goes to the very heart of worship. Even many in the body of Christ have surrendered to the idea that the good life is found in the accumulation of possessions, power, prestige or pleasure we can attain in this age. One of my goals is to make the word of God applicable to our daily lives. One way you can look at the "whore of Babylon" in Revelation is simply as a picture of apostate humanity being seduced by a system which seeks to make god out of this present age under the domain of darkness.

In looking at generalities, four major powers have greatly affected the direction of history: the Military, Religion, Politics and Economics. You can find examples where the following generalities do not apply, but overall history has followed these four major powers.

The world was ruled with Military might until the end of the Roman Empire. At the collapse of the Roman Empire religion through the Catholic Church, Orthodox Church and Islam ruled the world through religion. The Catholic Church, during the Middle Ages, ruled the West with complete dominance.

I don't think we realize in our day the power the church held during the Dark Ages. The details of life were controlled by the priest's and the church even dictated to kings. The Protestant Reformers were historicist (To better understand the term historicist refer to Appendix A at the back of book) in their view of the book of Revelation who identified the Catholic Church as the whore of Babylon and the Pope as the Antichrist.

The Renaissance and Protestant Reformation broke the stranglehold of religion as a dominant power over Western nations. The result was the rise of politics as the dominating power. In the 17th century politics gained the ascendancy of power in Europe and the decline of power culminated with WWII. Since WWII, the dominating power through which politics, religion and military operate their influence is through economic power. Economic power is to be the dominating force at the end of the age. Money is the motivating factor of many of our own decisions.

What makes economic power unique is that for the first time in history, organizations have arisen that have both the ideology and the technology to bring about one world. In Revelation 17:18, it states that "the woman whom you saw is the great city, which reigns over the kings of the earth."

[9] "When empire was embodied in clearly defined entities like nation-states, it was relatively easy to trace the contours of imperial power. Global capital, however, is a more elusive reality. Nonetheless, it may be startling to see how precisely

the reality of global capital matches both that of the Roman
Empire in particular and Revelation's wider critique of empire
generally."

In Revelation 18:11-16 we can see that Babylon is the center of
commerce. However, Babylon is not only about economic power,
but also about culture if you look at Rev. 18:22 where it speaks of
music. Look at how world culture is being connected by music.
Media Corporations are some of the largest, like Sony and Virgin,
affecting the populations of the world, not to mention the entire
multi-billion-dollar business coming out of Hollywood, and the
media empires being built in Europe and Asia. It has been said that
sex is a universal language, but it could also be said of music. The
power of music and its influence upon culture cannot be understated.
Culture affects the way we live, think and act. However, the
commerce generated by the 'spirit of Babylon' is corrupt and
corrupting, characterized by materialism without morality, pleasure
without purity, wealth without wisdom, lust without covenant love. It
is a culture of corruption; however the smile of the harlot is
peculiarly appropriate, giving anyone what they want in exchange for
money. It is what John called the lust of the flesh, lust of the eyes
and the pride of life (I John 2:1-7) or the spirit of this age (To get
additional details on this subject go to www.foundationpub.org
Lesson 10: A Lifestyle of Repentance).
In looking at the materialism promoted in Western culture, it
would be hard to ignore at least a link to the influence of the 'spirit of
Babylon'. Where do we get the tremendous drive in modern culture
towards materialism, hedonism, and pursuing a life of ease with
pleasure? It would be hard not to see a connection to the 'Babylon'
spoken of in Revelation. In Revelation 18:3 we are told "the
merchants of the earth have become rich by the wealth of her
sensuality." "Wealth" is the Greek word *dunamis*, a noun, which
means "power, strength, and ability." In this text it refers to the
power and strength of Babylon to seduce the nations of the earth.
"Sensuality" is a Greek word meaning "arrogant or
unrestrained luxury." The spirit of Babylon, with its worship of
money and power, will promote and push unrestrained luxury,
sensuality, and pleasure designed to develop an all-consuming
power over the masses via their uncontrolled lust patterns. It
promotes the false ideas that our significance, security, and

fulfillment are attained by the abundance of the things we possess in luxury, comfort and pleasure, etc. It is an all-consuming culture of covetousness organized in opposition to God.

Paul told the believing "wheat" of the kingdom to, "consider the members of your earthly body as dead to immorality, impurity, passion, evil desire, and **greed, which is idolatry**" (Colossian 3:5: Emphasis mine). The Greek word for greed in this text is pleonexia and is best translated covetousness. It is defined as 'the desire for having more or for what he has not. It is said to be the root of the works of the flesh. It is the longing of the creature which has forsaken God to fill itself with lower objects of nature."

Paul equates covetousness as being the exact same expression as bowing down and worshiping an idol. We have equated worship with a service where music is played, but worship could more simply be defined as whatever has control over your thoughts and hearts. Worshipping idols is allowing your heart to be taken away from Christ as the center. It is what we give our time, money and heart to.

[10] "Did you know that the thing from which you derive the most pleasure is the very thing you worship? It could be wicked or a mundane thing. But ask yourself: where do you find the most irresistible pleasure? That is what you worship."

I am not saying you shouldn't buy nice things, enjoy this life or even live in a nice house etc. However, we can look around our society, and possibly our own lives, to see that we have been worn out by the attractions and excesses of a culture focused on material wealth and carnal pleasure (food, sports, entertainment and sex).

Material possessions or physical enjoyments are not evil, but we must make sure we apply self-control and are not dominated by anything other than the cross of Christ and the presence of His Spirit. It is wise to look at our culture and realize that our definition of moderation in the West is excess to ninety percent of the rest of the world. I am asking you if Christ is at the center of your heart and decision making? I am asking you if you are spending time being transformed by the word and Spirit of Christ or is the surrounding culture around you molding you?

[11] "Pursuing the pleasures of this world can become intoxicating. It is here where Satan's activity is most veiled.

Instead of seeking God and being available for His will, many of us are entangled in debt and desire. Like the ancient Babylonians, ours is a 'land of images, and [we] are mad over idols' (Jer. 50:38 Amplified). Many Christians are caught in a maze of distractions. Idolatry is so familiar to us, we think it not strange!"

It is important that we understand that the link or door to immorality is covetousness. It is the longing of the creature (man) which has forsaken God, or just set God aside for the moment, to fill itself with lower objects of nature. When we have reduced our identity to what we have or what we do instead of who we are in Christ, we are chasing after an idol. If any of this becomes our identity, then it can also become an idol that we serve, instead of our identity being Christ. The result will be that we are no longer living life from the center, and we have allowed the peripheral to crowd out the center, which is Christ in us.

I am not saying that the peripheral is not important, but if it becomes the center, then it is out of place and can become an idol. The point I am making is that we must put Christ and our worship of the Father as central to our life and decision making. The essence of the 'fear of the Lord' is to delight in the presence of the Spirit and being consumed with His purpose which will displace all idols as we become surrendered worshippers of our Father. If we are not consistent worshippers of our Father then we will allow idolatry to keep us from our purpose, ultimately leave us empty, lead to our destruction and keep us out of the kingdom of God.

If you are like me, then you sometimes, maybe more often than not feel overwhelmed by the system we live in. We have numerous payments just to make it through the month; then we contemplate saving for retirement, college for kids or for ourselves, the occasional car breakdown or problem with the house. On top of all the financial stress we face then we must learn to live with our spouses, children, co-workers, employers, neighbors and church body.

We are in this system; therefore, we need wisdom to navigate through life's circumstances. Wisdom can be defined as the ability to relate with God and others. It can also be defined as the ability to do the right thing at the right time, or the understanding of what to avoid doing. Proverbs defines wisdom as the principle thing or the main thing.

Wisdom laid the foundations of the world (Prov. 8:29-30) and wisdom will help us build our lives (Prov. 9:1) with Christ as the center. Life has no meaning, no purpose and void without Christ. You know by now that with Christ, life is not going to be easy, but if we keep Him as our center then we live life with purpose. It is only through Him that we can truly find meaning, and if we will ask for His wisdom, then He will give us what we need to fulfill our journey.

All I will say is that a simple life based on godliness and contentment is better than the slavery of debt. I know it is not popular, but Paul did say that "we brought nothing into the world, and we can take nothing out of it. But if we have food and clothing, we will be content with that" (I Timothy 6:7-8). In Luke 12:15 Jesus said, "Take heed and keep yourselves from all covetousness: for a man's life consist not in the abundance of things which he possesses." I am not advocating taking a vow of poverty to demonstrate your godliness. Humility of heart, not lack of finances is a kingdom attribute and it is learning the place of contentment in our covetous culture that helps our hearts become free.

Contentment helps keep us from being taken over with covetousness. Contentment actually means to be satisfied. It is the language that Jesus used when speaking about how the Father will provide for His children (Matthew 6:24-27) telling them they don't have to worry and toil, but they also may not get everything they want. A little Rolling Stones wisdom applies here in the lyric, "You can't always get what you want, but you might find sometimes you get what you need."

If we don't learn the power of contentment, then we are never going to have the true financial blessing the Father intends for our lives: finances that bless our lives without corrupting our hearts. It is important that we don't twist the teaching on prosperity, or the blessing of God into an idol that takes possession of our hearts, instead of blessing our lives so that we can be a blessing to others. You may be going through a difficult time where you are actually having to rely on others, so be thankful for God's provision in every season of your lives.

As a New Covenant priest, part of our service is using our gifts and abilities to make a living. We are all called as priests to offer up the sacrifice of giving by using our material wealth to help others, give to the poor and provide finances for the spreading of the gospel.

Certain individuals in the body of Christ will have an extraordinary gift of giving (Romans 12:8), and will be channels for large amounts of money so that the message of the gospel can be spread. The kind of individuals the Spirit will use in this service will be tried and tested through fires so that they can be channels of blessing, and not reservoirs of greed.

I have learned the freedom to not have to compare myself with others financially; Paul said that he learned to be content in whatever circumstance in which he found himself. He said, "I know how to get along with humble means, and I also know how to live in prosperity" (Philippians 4:12). We need the freedom to understand that we are simply a part; therefore, we should not be afraid to be ourselves and give others the liberty to discover the path God has called them to follow.

If we don't have a strong identity in Christ, then we will easily be taken captive by the identity presented to us from others, and even taken captive by the identity of covetousness presented to us from the Babylonian ideas that have saturated our culture. Enslavement to the opinion of others is the source of bondage in modern society. We need to make sure that our actions are prompted by the Spirit of Christ instead of what others may say or think. As a New Covenant priest, we have a unique part to play in the kingdom of God.

The scriptures are full of paradoxes. The reality is, truth is often realized by maintaining a tension between two opposite truths revealed in the word of God. The scriptures clearly indicate that we can enjoy material things and our Father wants to not only bless us with His Spirit, but also with His provision.

The material world is good, but it is limited. To deny God's material provision in this world is to be an ascetic, but to put your trust in what the Bible calls 'uncertain riches' (I Timothy 6:17) is to be a materialist. We are to be content, but always pressing forward into God's purpose, resting in His provision to fulfill His will.

WHO IS GOING TO INFLUENCE YOU?

As previously stated, this book is not an exhaustive interpretation of the book of Revelation, but I hope that you are able to see what is happening in our modern world and how to relate it to our walk with

God in regards to worship. I do hope that you will spend some time looking at the appendix provided at the end of this book so you can understand differing views of how to interpret the book of Revelation. I give you the five main views so you can have a better understanding of how people form their opinions, but I don't take a hard line on what I consider to be debatable areas of scripture. I follow the policy that "in essentials UNITY, in non-essentials liberty, in all things charity." Another wise little word is say is to "Major on majors and minor on minors".

As I said my goal in writing is to make the word of God practical to our everyday lives. Understanding the Bible in a practical way should affect our conduct. George Barna has done research showing that many times you cannot distinguish American Christians from unbelievers in moral issues like lying, stealing, and adultery. It is for this reason that we are called to make disciples, not just converts, teaching them to observe everything that the Lord has commanded us to obey in day-to-day living.

The building of the tower of Babel was an attempt to be a 'gate way to god' and replace surrendered worship to the true God with a last ditch effort by fallen men to build God out of this world. In the same way, the woman on the scarlet beast entices men away from the worship of God with the promise of wealth, power, luxury, pleasure and religion. The end result is a mixture or confusion which leads to idolatry.

The city set on a hill, the bride of Christ, is supposed to be the antithesis to the spirit Babylon, but many times the church has the same type of mixture. Instead of being a light to the world we are the color gray full of a postmodern mixture. Instead of relying on the power of God by faith like Abraham; looking for the city of God, we have many times settled in the plains of Sodom. We have taken the easy and popular way like Lot; instead of separating ourselves from the corruption of this age.

The church Paul wrote to in the first century found itself in the midst of a society given to idolatrous worship practices. Paul told them to "COME OUT FROM THEIR MIDST AND BE SEPARATE," (II Corinthians 6:17). John in the Revelation used similar language in referring to the Babylonian system by saying, "Come out of her, my people" (Revelation 18:4).

Paul understood that we could live in the world while at the same time be separate. In looking at the text of Corinthians, we get a glimpse at what Paul was saying. He was not saying to cut your self off from the outside world. If you lived during the Roman Empire, do you think you could cut yourself out of that society? No, but you better understand that just because you live in Rome does not mean you act like the Romans.

I lived in Canada outside of Toronto, just north of Lake Erie for two years. In that area the soil is very fertile and the religious community of the Dutch Mennonites settled the area. You can still go through this area and see them riding horse and buggy on the side of the road, having built an entire culture separate from the surrounding modern world.

Paul was not saying that we cannot go to a secular college, or that we could not work in a corporation. He was not saying that we could not be business owners making a good living, a famous musician, or even a politician etc. Paul was saying don't operate by the same spirit as the Babylonian system of covetousness and immorality. Don't operate by the works of the flesh. Paul was saying that our primary allegiance must be our covenant with Christ. If Christ is not our central focus then when the pressure comes we will bow to other objects to fill the void.

We have to deal with this world until Christ returns and we should set examples like Daniel. Daniel lived in the heart of Babylonian power, yet he was not partaking of the spirit of Babylon, but lived a life dedicated to worshipping God. Daniel was a man of prayer, dedicated to the word of God, and full of the Spirit of wisdom.

As New Covenant priests it is part of our worship to have a great work ethic, be easy to get along with, have a positive attitude, and set an example of godliness. At the same time, we must be a people of the word and prayer, dedicated to worship. Our lives may be the only Bible that anyone ever reads. We need to understand that the decisions we make in business and life should reflect that we are worshippers of the Father. Even if we don't realize it our actions, conduct and decisions are based on who or what we worship. We reflect through our lives the object or objects that we worship.

The book of Revelation identifies Babylon as a 'whore'. The image implies infidelity to one's covenant partner, Christ Himself, while at the same time implying intimacy and union with the world.

The power of Babylon is the power of seduction in drawing people away from the true worship of the Father in Spirit to the lowly road of idolatry.

God wants us to prosper which is to help us get along in our journey of faith; however material wealth is never to be our goal. In speaking about prosperity, A.W. Tozer said that God "will not aid men in the selfish striving after personal gain. He will not help men to attain ends which, when attained, usurp the place He by every right should hold in their interest and affection." What Tozer is saying is that it is not the Spirit of God which is drawing you away to a pursuit of power, attaining wealth or sensuality.

Tozer was not saying that we cannot be successful in business, education, entertainment, sports etc. He is saying that it is not the Spirit of God that would have you pursue the things of this world, thinking that true satisfaction can be attained by gaining this world, whether in ministry or business. Jesus asked, "What benefit is it to gain the world and lose our soul?" We need to be the best at whatever gifting God has given us, and as stewards we are held responsible to be faithful to use our abilities, however our identity is to be Christ not what we do or what we have. Michael L. Brown in his book 'Revolution' says,

> "We must demonstrate the real meaning of life and articulate the true purpose of our existence, making it clear that our lives are not measured by the abundance of our possessions (see Luke 12:15) or by being somebody great in the eyes of man (see I Cor. 3:18,19) or by having earthly success or achievements (see Her, 9:23, 24). The real meaning of life is to know Jesus and to make Him known (see John 17:3; Acts 20:24). Apart from knowing Him and making Him known, our lives are empty, aimless, and worthless."

Idolatry is not simply falling down to worship a statue or tree. Rather, the issue in the old covenant with Israel, and today with the true church is that of entering into covenant with the fellow inhabitants of the land and adopting their worship and culture.

We have been called to be witnesses of the resurrection life of Christ, which means our lives are to be marked as distinct and set apart. I am not talking about spiritually weird, but if we are in a relationship with the life of God, then our lives should demonstrate the fruit of that life.

I was saved during my first semester of college, and I was greatly affected by two believers in my classes who displayed the life of the Spirit. It was not what they said, but it was who they were or the life of Christ displayed in their lives. Idolatry is the act of being conformed to this world while rejecting the transforming power of the Spirit. Paul in II Corinthians 6:14-16 asks several questions:

> "Do not be bound together with unbelievers; for what partnership have righteousness and lawlessness, or what fellowship has light with darkness? Or what agreement has the temple of God with idols?"

If you look at the book of Daniel you will find that he, along with his friends, serve as an example to the end-time believer; that in the midst of Babylon we can be separate, not bowing down to the idolatrous worship. We can be set apart by the Spirit of God in the midst of a perverse generation to worship God in spirit and truth. In the midst of a covetous society given over to extremes of luxury, immorality, sensuality, and false religion, Daniel humbled himself under the power of the Spirit. As a result of his humility and faith, God gave him wisdom to overcome, along with power to influence ungodly kingdoms.

Peter said that we are merely pilgrims and foreigners in this present evil age until the return of Christ. Therefore, we should live with a stronger view of the city whose builder and maker is God. It is only by living the life of the Spirit that we are going to truly demonstrate or be witnesses of the gospel of the kingdom.

It is of utmost importance that we gain a clear understanding of true worship so that we are not taken captive by the seducing power of Babylon in the times in which we live. We must allow that power of the risen Christ to purge our hearts from covetousness as we surrender all to Him so that we are those who worship in spirit and in truth.

Chapter 3
WORSHIP AND THE HEART

"The twenty-four elders and the four living creatures fell down
and worshiped God who sits on the throne saying, "Amen
Hallelujah."
~**Revelation 19:4**~

When I mention the word worship what picture comes into
your mind? To many in the modern church when the word worship
is mentioned, we immediately think of a service where the focus is
music and singing. I am not saying this is totally incorrect, but the
view is limited in its outlook concerning biblical worship.

Worship is greatly enhanced by music and singing to become
an expressive action. The simple definition of the word worship in
both the Old and New Covenants simply means to bow down or to
be humble before someone as an act of respect before a superior
being. I define true worship as the rule of the Spirit of God
inhabiting the heart of man, where expressive acts of godly service
are performed in complete surrender to the Father. Yes, this includes
such acts as bowing down in humility of heart or lying prostrate
before the presence of the Lord, but is not limited to such actions.

As I have already said, we live in a day when many things are
trying to rule over our hearts. It is important that we understand that
it is not a building from which God is seeking worship, but the
Father is seeking worship from our hearts. John 4:23 states that our
Father God is seeking true worshipers. He is not looking for the
burning of incense or the chanting of songs. He is not looking for
the blood of bulls or goats. He is not looking for a specific race,
gender or color of people. God is looking for hearts in all nations
that are dedicated and offered up to Him in true worship so that He

can inhabit and dwell as a Father in the hearts of His sons and daughters.

Let's take a look at the context of John 4 so that we can see the dramatic transition that Christ brought in regards to the way in which man would relate to the Father in regards to worship. The scene is set on a dry day in Samaria in a city called Sychar at Jacob's well, the son of the patriarch Abraham. Jesus was tired and thirsty so he sat down by the well alone while His disciples went into town to get food. The story starts with a Samaritan woman coming to the well and Jesus asking her for a drink.

To say that the Jews and Samaritans had their differences regarding the facts of the way to worship would be an understatement. To begin with, the Jews regarded the Samaritans as an inferior race. In the same way that Gentiles were regarded as unclean based on their race, the Samaritans were considered half- breeds, and looked at as worse than dogs by the Jews. Indeed, they had no dealings with one another and were separated by many centuries of deep hostility. However, the root of the problem was not just lineage, but over the way they both viewed worship.

[1] "The Samaritans had built their own temple on Mt. Gerizim, where they offered sacrifices according to their understanding of the Law...they believed that they had access to a means of acceptable sacrifice, validated by a long historical tradition, which gave them a legitimate claim on the God of Israel. From a Jewish perspective, this worship could never have been correct under any circumstances."

The rift between Jews and Samaritans was one of race, ritual and location. It is through the Jews that redemption has entered the world. Abraham, the father of our faith and of the Jewish nation, was separated from his family and called to the worship of Jehovah. The covenant made with Abraham separated him from all the nations of the earth, and his physical lineage became God's nation among the nations to be Jehovah's chosen people.

[2] "This nation, according to God's Word, will be "My own possession among all the peoples…a kingdom of priests and a holy nation" (Exodus 19:5-6). Thus, the very fabric of humanity was rent at that moment, as the Lord God separated unto Himself a people who would be different, somewhat exclusive, and set apart for a specific purpose…This nation was the sole recipient of the revelations of God – His favor, His blessing, and His chastisement. All other nations, in fact the rest of the human race could relate to and interact with the God of creation through the agency and mediation of Israel alone."

Israel was given the word of God, the temple, and the prescribed pattern of worship. The entire nation of Israel was to govern its social, political, economic dealings and worship around the law given to Moses. A departure from the prescribed pattern of law was the basis of punishment and even death. The Jewish nation was instituted by God to be a vehicle to display His glory to the nations and be His own special people in the earth. It is in this context of Jewish and Samaritan worship that we need to take a look at the encounter of Jesus and the Samaritan woman.

Worship in Spirit and Truth

Jesus' encounter with the Samaritan woman at the well was significant to give us an understanding that Christ redefines worship. In the time of the Bible, getting water was a necessity of daily life and something the women did in the early hours of the morning before the heat of the day. It was a social occasion for the women of the village where they would exchange news and interact. The woman in this story was at the well in midday, and alone, which lets us know she was a shunned woman.

Jesus asks her for a drink and the encounter begins. "The Samaritan woman, taken aback, asked, 'How come you, a Jew, are asking me, a Samaritan woman, for a drink?' (Jews in those days wouldn't be caught dead talking to Samaritans.)" (John 4:9 The Message) Jesus then begins to tell her about the living water he has available to quench her true thirst. When she requests to receive this gift, he then begins to draw her out to face the necessity of repentance so that she could receive the gift of Living Water.

The first step to worship is a heart turned in true

repentance. When Jesus walked this earth during His ministry, He was the apostle, prophet, evangelist, pastor and teacher. In this text, we see Jesus the prophet who begins to read the woman at the well's innermost thoughts so that truth could be in her heart.

The prophetic gift in the church is important. The gift is not to be over emphasized in neglect to the other gifts but has a place. We are told not to despise prophecy (I Thess. 5:20). Paul in his epistle to the Corinthians places a high premium on having the prophetic ministry operating among the people of God so that the secrets of people's hearts can be disclosed. Paul says that the purpose is so that people will worship God (I Corinthians 14:25).

In I Corinthians 14:1 Paul says that we are to earnestly desire the Spirit's manifestations. The revelatory gifts or manifestations of the Spirit are the word of knowledge, word of wisdom and discerning of spirits operating in the midst of our assemblies. This is one of the equipping purposes of the prophetic.

At the same time, the saints should be equipped to be a prophetic people, revealing to the world the heart of the Father. I am no way looking at all the aspects of prophetic ministry in this chapter, but I hope to lay down some parameters so that we can properly relate to those with prophetic gifts (In my free online school of discipleship www.foundationpub.org you will get more detail on the subject of the 'gift of the prophet' found in Ephesians 4:11, 'gift of prophecy' in Romans 12:6 and the 'manifestation of prophecy' in I Cor. 12:10).

I spent some time in Queens, New York working with a church planting team. On one occasion, I spent the night at the location where we were holding meetings. I woke up in the middle of the night and I was thirsty, so I went down the street corner where there was an all night store open. You could not go in, but there was a window where you could buy things.

As I was standing there, two women walked up carrying bundles of newspapers. I sparked up a conversation when one of the women began telling me she was a Christian. At that moment, the word of knowledge manifested, and I told her that she had stolen the papers she had and she was going to use the money to buy drugs. She immediately went into a rage and started cursing me. I had finished what I was sent to do, so I turned around and walked back to our meeting place to go back to sleep. The whole time I was walking back this woman was yelling down the street at me.

Two weeks later, I was ministering at the Sunday morning service. People came up to the front and I was praying over them. One of the women asked me if I remembered her. I did not, but then she reminded me of that night and oh, what a difference I noticed! The glory of God was on this same woman's face.

God uses the prophetic gift to cut to the heart so true change can happen and not just artificial repentance. I would advise you to make sure you are moving by the Spirit in such a situation and understand how to deliver each word in the manner that the Father desires. In this instance, this woman needed an abrupt, confrontational word to break through the darkness over her life. It is not always the case, so you have to be sensitive to the Spirit's leading.

The prophetic and the evangelistic gifting have many similarities, which will cause them to operate in the same function at times. However, the main difference is that the evangelist is gifted to reach the lost while prophets have a more foundational function in establishing the church. It is best if they both work with apostolic teams, and it is imperative that they equip believers to function in their particular gifting.

Where there is no manifestation of the Spirit then the people of God will surely be given to false worship since their hearts will be veiled with hidden sin. You may have the prophetic ministry operating in your midst and not call it that, but without the power of the Spirit you simply have a form of godliness with no transforming power to change the heart.

Jesus so poetically said when we act this way we become like white washed tombs: religious people who look clean on the outside, but the inside, there is no life of the Spirit. The prophetic gift is instrumental in confronting the traditions of men and religion, which we simply gravitate towards when we are not challenged to pursue God with our whole heart. Look at the first three chapters of the book of Revelation and you will see the prophetic gift in operation comforting, correcting and encouraging the church.

Prophets are foundational ministries used to establish believers in an understanding of covenant commitment to Christ. The prophetic gift also gives us a glimpse of heaven, seeing beyond this natural realm into the spiritual. In addition, the gift is used to help identify gifting in people's lives, motivate them to use them, and help to establish correct ministry motives so that what we build is in alignment with the heart of the Father.

The woman, once confronted with her sin, then turns to the question of worship. If Jesus could read her heart, could he not then answer the question of worship, which separated Jews and Samaritans for centuries? Jesus gave her a revolutionary answer and redefines the entire focus of worship.

> "Jesus said to her, 'Woman believe Me, an hour is coming when neither in this mountain, nor in Jerusalem, shall you worship the Father.
>
> You worship that which you do not know; we worship that which we know, for salvation is from the Jews. But an hour is coming, and now is, when the true worshipers shall worship the Father in spirit and truth; for such people the Father seeks to be His worshipers.
>
> God is Spirit and those who worship Him must worship in spirit and truth.'" (John 4:21-24)

Jesus' answer was that the Samaritans did not have a clue about true worship. In addition, He declared that the Jews only had a partial revelation of worship instituted by the Law of Moses, which was merely transitory.

Jesus redefined worship by declaring that it was no longer a matter of *location* and *ritual*, nor did a person's *racial* history make any difference. The New Covenant and its new worship instituted by Christ have been instituted for all nations. However, the center of worship is no longer captive to a physical location in the earth, but the earthen vessel of man is now a habitation of the Spirit of the Living God.

It was revolutionary to speak in such terms. The Jews spent centuries worshiping under the prescribed manner of the Law. Now the Messiah in whom the promise of Abraham was fulfilled was saying the hour has arrived to break out of the box of the Law and its restricted worship.

The first martyr of the church Stephen declared:

> "The Most High does not dwell in houses made by human hands; as the prophet says:
> 'Heaven is my throne, and earth is the footstool of my feet; what kind of house will you build for me? Says the Lord." (Acts 7:49)

How could we ever think that God could be put into a box? He is not bound to any geographical location; God is Spirit. In the same way that Babylon is connecting the nations together in antithesis, the Spirit of God is the common source of the body of Christ throughout the nations of the earth.

It was on the day of Pentecost when the church was birthed with the Holy Spirit that the confusion brought at the tower of Babel was broken when the One New Man (the church made up of both Jew and Gentile with Christ as head) in the earth was born from above.

At Babel, God confused man's language, but on the day of Pentecost, by the power of the Spirit, all who have been born from above, through Christ's blood covenant, have been united together by the unity of the Spirit. It is only through the Spirit that we can be the true worshipers that the Father is seeking. However, to fully have the Spirit, we must also embrace with our whole hearts the truth. Paul said that in the last day's men would be *lovers of pleasure more than lovers of God* (II Timothy 3:4).

Postmodernism has saturated our age and even affected the church. [3] "Relativism has its typical catchphrases. 'That may be true for you, but not for me.' 'It all depends on how you look at it.' 'Nothing is black and white.' Thus adultery, like beauty, is reduced to a function of the eyes of the beholder and sodomy is reduced to an 'alternative lifestyle.' All values and judgments dissolve into a pervasive gray haze. That grayness is fatal to truth. It is the result of practicing relativism and mixing right and wrong, white, and black, light and dark."

If we want to be the type of worshipers that the Father is seeking to have intimate fellowship with, then we must become lovers of the truth. When Jesus confronted the woman with her sin, she did not run away from the light but allowed the light to penetrate the darkness of her heart. In the same way, we must allow the Spirit to penetrate the innermost being of our hearts so that we have truth in our innermost being.

David, the most vivid picture of a man after God's own heart in the Old Testament, wrote Psalm 51. He wrote this Psalm after Nathan, the prophet confronted him about his covetous action of adultery and murder. David, like most of us, hid from his own heart, but when confronted, he repented and wrote that God desires truth in our innermost being, and wisdom in our hidden parts. "'If it is not there, we are false, despite all of our outward professions. Truth is a spirit; it has to do primarily with our spirit, our heart, our innermost being. To walk in truth is to walk in and by the Spirit of Truth."

If we receive the Spirit and allow truth to dwell in our innermost being, then we will become the habitation of the Spirit, and will be sons of God who have intimate fellowship with the Father. False worship or idolatry will never satisfy the deep longing of man's heart, but only an open heart filled with the Spirit can produce the type of intimacy for which man is searching. Covetousness fills the heart with earthly worship but leaves our hearts thirsty. Covetousness leaves our hearts like the U2 lyric, "I still haven't found what I'm looking for."

Worship's Hindrances: Legalism and Lawlessness

Like the man and woman in the garden, when the Spirit exposes sin, the human tendency is to cover it up or make excuses for why you are the way you are. Religion is a substitute for true worship. The strength of religion is found in legalism, or its antithesis, lawlessness. If you look at the writings of the New Testament, you will attest to the fact that it is these two realities that form the greatest battle to a heart dedicated to Christ. However, if you get down to the root of the issue they come from the same source. The tree of the knowledge of good and evil is one tree with two results. I hear it all the time. It's only white magic. Whether it is white or black it comes from the same satanic source.

Legalism can be defined in many different ways. "Restrictive" would be one way that we can define the word. The woman at the well understood that, in her day, there were restrictions to worship in regards to *ritual, location* and *race.* Do we have any man-made restrictions on worship in regard to ritual and location today?

When I mention the word church, what is the first picture that pops into your mind? If you are like most people, then the picture of a physical building pops into your mind. It may be an old white building with a steeple, an old cathedral or the dressed-up metal buildings of our modern places where believers gather.

I am not in any way opposing the cultural norms that we have developed in regard to church buildings. However, there are great numbers of believers worldwide meeting together for fellowship in variety of ways outside of traditional formats. The 'Missional Movement', which includes various forms of church life, is restoring many positive aspects to people's faith.

Practically speaking many are following these "new paradigms" of organizational structure based on the cost savings of not having to maintain buildings or sharing facilities among multiple congregations. In addition, it gives a congregation the flexibility of not being tied down to one place. I am in no way saying that by simply throwing off cultural norms you are actually entering into true worship. At the same time, many believers meet in what we label "church buildings" and many have a true understanding of worship not being bound by ritual or location.

I am challenging the mentality that worship is defined as a certain type of style and restricted to a certain physical location. It has been my experience, and if you look historically at the church anytime we think that we have God boxed in, He breaks out of our restrictions. In addition, worship style can vary depending on a group's preference and the cultural setting (Ex. In a rural setting people may tend to be more conservative in style than we find in a progressive city setting. The same applies to ethnic varieties of expression and then you just have different genres of music).

We need basic guidelines, but the bottom line is that it is *the presence of the Spirit, which is the distinguishing mark of true worship.* Worship style and physical location is irrelevant if it does not have the distinguishing mark of the Spirit! If we want to be true worshipers, then *we must be carriers of the presence of the Spirit in our daily lives and corporate gatherings,* since it is only the Spirit which sets us apart to be the children of God.

When we dislocate our worship from everyday life then it is possible to have a stronger identity and dedication to supporting a system of worship instead of living a life of worship. As a result, *far too many believers have a stronger identity to a physical location and style of worship instead of the person of Christ.* The unintended consequences are a replacement of the presence of the Spirit in our lives to ritualism. It is important that we maintain a holistic approach to worship that affects every area of our lives and is not restricted to a certain style (ritual) or location so that we are carriers of the presence of the Spirit. True revival is the church impacting all facets of society because we are carriers of the Spirit wherever we go.

One of the main things that keep us from the presence of the Spirit is legalism. Legalism restricts, judges anything outside of established norms (sectarianism) and proposes exclusion for those who refuse to submit. I spent years judging others for not following certain styles of praise or ideas of church life. I still have my preferences when it comes to a certain corporate worship style and church life, but I realize it is my preference, so I give others the freedom to choose their preferred style.

It seems that we have allowed divisiveness to enter into our worship of the Father, which should unite us. I am not talking about uniting around a particular style, but united around our surrendered humility of heart in worship of our one Father. We can all learn from one another and no group has a monopoly on how to worship the Father since we are each unique. Legalism causes us to judge by externals and put confidence in our own ability. Legalism is a religious critical attitude no matter what form it takes.

If we are filled with the Spirit, then we are going to give others the liberty to follow the Spirit. Jesus was not just filled with truth, but He was also filled with mercy. The Holy Spirit does not just convict of sin, but He also liberates the heart with freedom and flexibility. We need to give one another the freedom and flexibility to be themselves. The Holy Spirit uses many types of vehicles or ministries to reach people. The Spirit filled body of Christ is diverse, and if we are filled with the Spirit, we will recognize Christ in all of His fullness.

I have even seen believers become worshippers of the written word to the point of restricting the presence and power of God in our hearts and corporate gatherings. I had a friend who was ministering in India and the people were treating the Bible as an idol. To illustrate, while he was preaching, he threw the Bible down and stood up on it. That did not go over really well, but the point is that the Bible is surely God's inspired word, but the real word is the person of Christ. The written word is important, but the goal is to bring us into a personal relationship with the 'Living Word'.

The Pharisees' were a picture of legalism. When we put a premium on style, outward appearance and legal form, then we have departed from the Spirit of liberty. Paul in opposing the legalist trying to bring external form over believers, states, "we are the true circumcision, who worship in the Spirit of God and glory in Christ Jesus and put no confidence in the flesh." (Philippians 3:3) If anyone had a right to boast in lineage, dedication to ritual, and adherence to being a true Jew who adhered to temple worship, it was Paul.

At the same time, Paul fought legal restrictions trying to produce an external form of ritual and location; he was not advocating lawlessness. The body of Christ is not a free-for-all, with every man doing what is right in his own eyes. Paul in teaching about when we are assembled as a body in regard to spiritual gifts to "let all things be done properly and in an orderly manner." (I Corinthians 14:40)

Paul does not lay forth a particular style, but he does set the parameters that we should not have chaos. Our personal lives should have order, and our corporate gatherings need spiritual power, but cannot be without order. I am not speaking of a lack of corporate participation, but at the same time I am not talking about a free for all where anything goes. The churches (sanctified people not sanctified buildings) that Paul planted eventually developed elders or pastors, who were spiritual overseers, who were mature facilitators of orderly corporate worship. These leadership principles apply to us in varying contexts.

Regarding worship and lawlessness, I am going to define it as mysticism. Legalists exalt form over substance while mystics tend to exalt subjective experience over truth. In using the term mysticism, I am in no way discouraging the experiencing of visions, dreams, prophecy, angelic visitations and many other encounters that the Bible clearly demonstrates are to be activity for the Spirit- filled believer (Acts 2:16-21; Read all of Acts).

In looking at worship and lawlessness I am addressing the

issue of allowing these many times subjective experiences to determine our doctrinal positions. In Zechariah 2:9 we see a stone with seven eyes and then in Isaiah 11:2, in speaking about Christ he then lists the sevenfold anointing.

We looked at these two scripture references in chapter one of this book and from them we see that the foundation does not change, but the Holy Spirit anointing gives us fresh insight, new dimensions of understanding and depths of wisdom. The Holy Spirit enlightens our hearts, opens the eyes of our understanding and leads us into all truth, which is found in Christ. However, exalting subjective experience over the word of truth is a pathway to the spirit of error.

We can never promote experiencing the presence of God as a replacement to sound doctrine, but as an equal an equivalence to soundness of truth since Christ is both the **wisdom** and **power** of God. The Samaritans setup their own prescribed way to worship, which totally contradicted the pattern God established through His word. There are guidelines for true worship. The question is, "Who determines them?" The options are that individuals determine them for themselves, church traditions determine them, or the word of God determines the prescribed guidelines for worship.

If individuals determine the boundaries for themselves, then it would be left to each person's subjective opinion. It is easy to see that the result would be chaos, which is what Paul had to confront in Corinthians. Therefore, we can conclude that there are some basic guidelines in regard to corporate worship to keep us from a free-for-all.

As I have previously said that we all have traditions, which are simply established norms. Different parts of the diverse body of Christ have established long years of church traditions in regard to corporate worship. I am not going to oppose such styles, as long as they do not become fences or veils that keep us from the Spirit of God.

Worship is about entering into the presence of the Father through the one sacrifice of Christ by the descending power of the Spirit. If church traditions keep us from the Father, Son and Spirit, then it is time to replace those traditions, or at the least put them in their proper place, which is subservient to the Triune God, not the other way around.

A number of people would have us to believe that we need to

emphasize the Jewish aspects of Jesus if we really want to have a correct image of Him. At the same time, there are others who say that we need to see the African Jesus or the South American Jesus.

In Acts 10, we see that while in a trance the Spirit gave Peter an open vision demonstrating that the gospel is for all people and all nations no matter the ethnic background. It is interesting that it was actually during a time of prayer that the prophetic anointing opened up Peter's heart, and as a result a new field of souls was harvested. The Spirit transforms souls so that they can be used to reach more souls for the kingdom of God. Peter was not in a church building, but he was on a friend's house or outdoor porch and then he was invited into another home where all the people came to Christ.

I will agree that, to understand Christ's writings, we need to understand the context in which they were spoken. The context is Hebraic or Jewish, but we do not relate to the Jesus that walked the earth, but the resurrected Christ at the right hand of the Father. I have no problem with Messianic Christians, which are Jews that believe in Jesus; however, I do have a problem with trying to make Gentiles into Jews. This is the same fight the authors of the New Testament had if you read Romans, Acts, Galatians and other parts of the New Testament.

I see a valid place for, and support Israel since our Messiah will return to the Mount of Olives in the same way that He left (Acts 1:9-11). Romans 9-11 clearly demonstrates that once the fullness of the Gentiles has arrived, the focused attention will be upon the Jewish people. Jesus is going to rule the nations from Jerusalem during the millennial reign of Christ.

To not give the Jew his rightful place is anti-Semitic, but to over emphasize that place is antichrist. We are beginning to see the 'One New Man' (Ephesians 3:3-6) assembled, which is Jews and Gentiles joined together under the one covenant of Christ the Messiah. The church is a kingdom of priests 'called out' of all nations; therefore, our worship of Christ is not subject to the invalid arguments of race.

It really doesn't matter what color Jesus was and it doesn't matter what color you are. If you are focused around race, whether Jewish or any other race, you have been taken captive by idolatry. At the same time, if you have a cultural identity, it is okay to keep it and be who the Father has made you to be. All ethnic groups are going to come and worship before the Father in this age and the age to come since He loves diversity. However, we are to relate to the risen Jesus who broke the power of death and ascended to the right hand of the Father with all authority in heaven and earth. It was Paul who said in II Corinthian 5:16 that we are to no longer relate to Jesus after the flesh. He came in the flesh, but was resurrected with a new body, the first fruits of those who will be raised from the dead and we are to relate with the resurrected Christ.

The only boundary that we have for corporate worship is the word of God. Yet, if you study through the New Testament, you will soon discover that [5] "the same God who is so specific about things that matter to Him and that are important for us has provided few details about the logistics of Christian assemblies. That silence suggests that we have freedom to develop the means by which we act as a united body of disciples, as long as we perform the functions of God's chosen ones in ways that comply with His general guidelines of behavior and the functioning" body of priests.

In the next chapter, I lay down some basic guidelines in the word of God concerning corporate prayer, praise and giving which is part of our corporate worship. We can never move beyond the word of God and exalt our subjective experiences above what the word teaches. The word of God is to be our guide, but we should not allow it to restrict us into ritualistic legalism, which will hinder our creative expression. We have the liberty of the Spirit to be creative in our individual and corporate worship, if we are not violating the principles of God. If the Bible does not forbid activity, then we have the freedom to be ourselves.

Each culture, body of believers and individual has the liberty to express their uniqueness in how they worship the Father, expressing a heart of love, thanksgiving and good works. Our covenant with Christ is the central focus of true worship; however, as we experience a living reality of His presence, we will experience prophecy, visions, dreams and visitations of the Holy Spirit. However, power without wisdom can lead to mysticism and a departure from the foundation of our faith. We must be grounded in the wisdom of covenant to understand true worship.

The Prophetic Anointing Equips for Worship

Jesus said, "the way is broad that leads to destruction...and the way is narrow that leads to life." (Matthew 7:13) The harlot system of Babylon is a broad way where anything goes, especially if you can make a profit, but the end result is destruction. The role of the prophetic ministry historically in the Old Testament and in the New Testament for today has been a call to lead people away from the pathway of destruction to the narrow path of life or the life of covenant.

It is an oversimplification, but prophets in the Old and New Testaments deal with motives of the heart, and the end result is to bring forth a heart wholly dedicated to worshipping the Father. Reading on in Matthew 7, Jesus then goes on to talk about false prophets who appear to be harmless, but they have a problem with their hearts. Jesus said that they are inwardly ravenous, producing bad fruit and spreading bad seed. It was the manifestation of Jesus the prophet, which gave the woman at the well a true understanding of worship; however, false prophets will lead us to false ideas of worship. False prophets lead us away from the simplicity of our foundation in Christ. You can see this especially in the occult and false religions, but I have also seen this happen to those within the church.

In Revelation chapter two, Jesus told the church in Pergamum that there were those among them who held to the teaching of Balaam. Balaam had a prophetic gift, but it was adulterated for profit. His motives became adulterated and when that takes place the fruit is ungodly counsel. He told King Balak that through the seduction of women he could cause men to break covenant with God through sexual immorality and therefore weaken the nation.

One of the teachings of Balaam is the false teaching of grace as a license to sin. It is an attitude that we can mix with the sin of the world and not be contaminated. In addition, it is using your gift to manipulate others for profit instead of serving with your gift. A false prophet, like any false ministry, will always have ulterior motives.

It has been my experience that prophets go AWOL when they start promoting mystical visions as doctrine. The result is leading people away from a simple devotion to Christ. It can manifest itself in two ways: either as a total disregard for any standards and structure, or they begin to become legalistic and domineering. The ultimate goal of prophetic ministry is to bring believers into a deeper walk with Christ by equipping the body with the motivation of the

Spirit to fulfill the Father's heart.

The prophetic gift, like any other Ephesians four gifting, is to impart an aspect of Christ into the life of the believer. Christ the prophet is a foundational gift, which is supposed to lay a deep understanding of covenant relationship in the believer's heart. This must be foundational to the gifts of the Spirit in operation in our lives. The result will be a heart of worship dedicated and submitted to the Lordship of Christ so that when we operate in the gifts, we have pure motives.

The essence of wisdom understands intimacy and spiritual union, which is the result of covenant. Proverbs 9:10 states that the beginning of wisdom is the fear of the Lord, and the word "fear" simply means reverence. To have wisdom, we must have the reverence to put God first in our lives.

The narrow way of wisdom leads to life because wisdom reverences covenant. The only two traditions or rituals we are commanded to keep in the New Testament if you want to call them that; is water baptism and the keeping of the covenant meal. Water baptism resembles the marriage ceremony while communion is a display of our continued commitment to our covenant partner's death and resurrection, but also, to the community of covenant keepers.

It is the understanding that worship is both vertical in reverencing Christ, but also horizontal in serving others. Read through Proverbs 9 as wisdom is personified. It says that wisdom has "mixed her wine: She has also set her table..." She then says to, "Come, eat of my food, and drink of the wine I have mixed. Forsake your folly and live, and proceed in the way of understanding." The narrow way of life is abiding in Christ, our covenant partner, and communing with a heart of humility with His body.

In looking at the tabernacle of Moses, we can see that it was the center of worship for the Israelites. Moses was told to make it according to the pattern or blueprint that he was shown. One point I want to make about the tabernacle and that is that it was built by the enabling and equipping of the Holy Spirit upon men. God did not just come down and build it, but He partnered with frail humanity and blessed the works of man's hands. It says of the main man who constructed the tabernacle that he was filled "with the Spirit of God, in wisdom, in understanding and in knowledge and in all craftsmanship." (Exodus 35:31) In the same way, God is using the gift of the prophet, which is an anointed servant to build into the church a foundational wisdom of how to live a life governed by the Spirit.

God was showing us His wisdom, that He does not just want us to have a visitation, but He wants the intimacy and spiritual union of habitation. The tabernacle, unlike the Temple of Solomon, was always on the move with the cloud by day and fire by night, which symbolizes our lives being governed by the Spirit.

The Tabernacle of Moses along with David's Tabernacle points to this present age, which is the kingdom of God manifested in and through the church. However, the Temple of Solomon points to the outward manifestation of the millennial kingdom introduced at the return of Christ, which will be both visible and more permanent aspect of the kingdom of God centered in Israel.

Habitation in our own hearts and corporately is produced through the humility of wisdom. Jesus was baptized in the Jordan River, the lowest river on the face of the earth; literally 1,200 feet below sea level. If we want to have the Spirit upon our lives, then we have to learn to walk in the humility of total surrender. The Spirit of wisdom descends down from above and it is "pure, peaceable, gentle, willing to yield, full of mercy and good fruits, unwavering, without hypocrisy." (James 3:17)

When we think of prophets, we normally think of powerful manifestations of prophecy, visions, dreams and the word of knowledge. Powerful manifestations are part of the prophets calling, but an important virtue we many times overlook is the Spirit of wisdom manifested through the prophetic gift, which is foundational in building the church.

God sent Elijah to bring the nation of Israel, who had apostatized to false worship, back to covenant. The central problem Elijah faced was a people who had departed from an understanding of covenant to the false worship of idolatry. If you look at all of the Old Testament prophets, you see a clarion call to repentance and a return to the God of covenant. Elijah understood covenant and any true prophet will understand the covenant of Christ and minister out the heart of the Spirit of Christ.

The purpose of the spiritual manifestations through the prophetic ministry is to bring you into a deeper respect for the work of Christ and produce a deeper worship of the Father in your heart. If a prophet's gift is not producing this fruit, then you have a right to question the gift and motivation. The word of God says do not despise prophesying (I Thessalonians 5:20-22), but it also says we need to test every prophecy, vision or dream. The reason we test prophetic experiences is because within a prophecy, vision or dream is the power to reproduce after its kind. It is the spirit behind the words that gives them life or death. Look at Acts 16:16-18 and you will see that the words of this fortune-teller were correct, but the spirit behind the words was demonic.

It has been my experience that prophets, which do not have consistent fellowship in the context of a community of believer's can go off into error. The prophetic gift, if not tempered with much humility, will lead to abuse. A true prophet will be one who understands the humility of submitting to one another in the fear of the Lord. A prophet who does not mingle with the sheep in humility will become a predator who feeds on the sheep.

The problem with ministers falling into sin is not necessarily a lack of authoritarian accountability, but a lack of transparent fellowship with other believers. The prophetic gift is best nurtured, cultivated and matured in community. I have known those with prophetic gifts submitted to a presbytery without transparent fellowship end up in a ditch.

Accountability to a presbytery is good, but it is not a cure to keeping people from high altitude disintegration. Prophets experience highs, and if they do not understand the *humility of transparent fellowship found in community* then they will always depart from the pathway of life. *Humility of heart* helps you to *recognize your own frailties* keeping you from the sin of pride, which is the pathway to deception. In the life of community where humility is practiced there is room to learn, make mistakes, be corrected and grow in your gifting.

False prophets operate by a false wisdom, loving the preeminence, having influence over others, and turning hearts towards themselves; instead of turning them to a pure devotion and dependence on Christ. False prophets, and for that matter any false ministry, turns people to themselves so that they can use them for their own purpose.

Instead of walking in the humility of wisdom, false leaders are operating in the mystery of lawlessness. [6] "Spiritual wolves are with the sheep for one purpose to consume them. Spiritual wolves are not present with the sheep to help them even though that is what they may publicly present about themselves." If we adulterate our gift for money or power, then we become false inwardly and hurt the sheep we are called to benefit.

Paul in giving qualifications for elders, or your group may call them pastors (local overseers), made one of the stipulations that they should be free from the love of money, and he also said they should not be domineering (I Timothy 3:3). He gave other character standards, but these two are very important.

When we are building through our own human ingenuity, strength and power inspired by the covetous spirit of Babylon, then we are operating in false wisdom. James says that when we have selfish ambition in our heart, we are arrogant (tares) and don't understand true worship. We are operating by the spirit of Babylon, which is earthly, natural, demonic (James 3:15). Anyone who has had any ministry experience would be honest and say that they have operated with the inspiration of false wisdom. However, a false prophet or any false ministry is one who does not have the humility to repent and allow the wisdom from above to create in him a true servants heart.

Music: The Motivation to Worship

The scriptures show a link between prophets, music and worship. Many of the songs recorded in Scripture were sung to the accompaniment of musical instruments. When David played, the prophetic anointing soothed Saul's tormented soul (I Samuel 16:23). The prophetic anointing came upon Elisha as a result of the playing of the stringed instrument (II Kings 3:14-15).

It is not my intention in this book to set forth any particular style of corporate worship, but I do want to show the important link between worship and music. The essence of worship has nothing to do with music, but the power of music can be used to enhance the worship experience. Music motivated the people to worship Nebuchadnezzar's idol in Babylon (Daniel 3:5) and when the music of the prophets played the Spirit came upon Saul, transforming him (I Samuel 10:6). In heaven right now, there is continuous worship before the throne (Revelation 5:9-14, 7:12-17, 11:17-18, 15:3-4 and 19:1-6).

To look around to find a link between music and the idolatrous worship of Babylon would not be hard to discover. I am no way saying that music performed by an unbeliever is evil. At the same time, just because it is a Christian performing does it mean that God is even involved?

Just as we can appreciate nature and the creation, we can appreciate and enjoy the gift that God has given to people in the form of the music they create. Music is a cultural phenomenon, which displays the soul of a people group. If you listen to Jewish, French, Caribbean music or that of any ethnicity, you get to taste the flavor of the people. We enjoy paintings and other artistic ability that non-Christians create, and we can enjoy their creative musical talent.

We become worldly not by engaging with the world, but by allowing it to shape our thinking. Jesus was clear about this in His prayer for his disciples when He said, "Not that you take them out of the world, but that you protect them from the evil one (John 17:15)."

> [6] "The art and music of nonbelievers, like the friendship of nonbelievers, could be a part of a process pressing us to conform to the 'pattern of this world' as Paul called it in Romans, but it doesn't have to be if we are being transformed through godly mind renewal. In fact, wrestling with worldly ideas is one way in which our minds are renewed. It challenges our assumptions and threatens our complacency."

It sends us back to the Bible and forces us to humble ourselves before God so that we can know the truth personally and apply that truth in a practical way.

Music is art, but it is spiritual art; therefore, we need to be aware that it can be inspired by demons to seduce and lead us away from Christ. Also, music can be inspired by the Spirit, which will always lead us to a deeper fellowship with Him.

> [8] "Music is one of mankind's fundamental avenues of communication, and one of the most successful because it transcends the conscious mind and reaches the subconscious…Music is 'heart to heart,' 'spirit to spirit.' That is why it is so destructive when used for evil. It touches the inner man."

Music has a transforming power to enhance our worship of the Father. God has gifted certain individuals with musical talent, however, without the Spirit of God empowering the musical talent; it is just talent. It is only the anointing of the Spirit, which has the power to destroy the enemies' hold over a person and change hearts to worship the Father. If the power of the Spirit is not present, then we are merely being entertained at best.

Paul said that when we come together as a 'New Covenant priesthood' that we each have something to give. It may be a teaching, encouraging word to a fellow warrior, a spiritual song etc. If we are a worshipping people, then when we come together for corporate worship, we will experience the Father's presence, and if unbelievers come in our midst, the Spirit will convict, reprove and show them their need of Christ.

Anointed music helps set aside worldly cares so that we can focus our attention on the Father. The power of identification should never be understated. We are all worshippers of something. It can be stated that there is no vacuum where worship does not exist and whatever we worship, we become like the object we behold. Engaging in false worship impacts our moral and spiritual condition in the same way when we are beholding a correct image of the Father we are changed. True worship produces the very character, nature and stability of the kingdom of God in our hearts since worship is the essence of Christ in us.

Jesus came to give us freedom from sin, slavery to the law, a heart of covetousness etc. Jesus gave the woman at the well that had no hope; hope to be free from the most divisive forces in society, which are race and religion. Her whole identification was that of a shunned woman; who was part of an inferior race with a flawed understanding of worship. I can only imagine the transformation her heart must have experienced as she identified with the message of true worship.

When we identify with ritual and location we are conformed to the image of religion or the lawlessness of unrestrained lust. The only power to transform is the descending power of the Spirit. The woman at the well was transformed when she acknowledged the truth concerning true worship by turning to the Lord. At that moment, the veil that had covered her heart was removed as she experienced for the first time in her life a heart of freedom overflowing with living water. Paul said that:

"Now the Lord is the Spirit; and where the Spirit of the Lord is there is liberty. But we all with unveiled face beholding as in a mirror the glory of the Lord, are being transformed into the same image from glory to glory just as from the Lord, the Spirit." (II Corinthians 3:17-18)

In this age we are going to constantly have pressure to conform to its morals, social norms opposed to the ways of God, and ethical lapses so commonly accepted. Just as Abraham looked for the city whose builder is God in like manner, we must realize that in this age we are simply pilgrims. We are not at home in this age; we are in transition. We must learn to embrace the Spirit daily so that we are transformed instead of conforming to the spirit of Babylon that continually tries to seduce our hearts away from true worship. Never let your hearts settle for merely the outward form of ritual and location, but long for an intimate relationship with your Father through the Spirit.

Chapter 4

A KINGDOM OF PRIESTS

"Worthy art thou to take the book and break its seals, for thou
hast been slain and by thy blood hast purchased for God men
from every tribe, and tongue, and people and nation! Thou hast
made them a kingdom of priests for our God..."
~Revelation 5:9-10~

The early church had an understanding of the entire church
being a kingdom of priests. Every member was identified as a
minister or servant with a gift. The two-tier system of saints divided
among the clergy and laity is also absent from the New Testament
writers. I do believe the tide is turning, but presently a majority of
Christian churches still see a division between "the ministers" and the
rest of the body:

[1] "In our time it may well be that the greatest single bottleneck
to the renewal and outreach of the church is the division of
roles between clergy and laity that results in hesitancy of the
clergy to trust the laity with significant responsibility, and in
turn a reluctance on the part of the laity to trust themselves as
authentic ministers of Christ, either in the church or outside of
the church."

As I have already said in this book, leadership is essential!
However, *leaders are simply mature facilitators* serving the flock with their
gifts who are supposed to encourage every other member to follow
their servant example. Jesus said that the greatest among
you is servant of all. True spiritual authority is based on serving and

relationship, unlike the gentile idea of authority, which is based on position. I am not saying that we don't have paid ministerial staffs, but I am saying that leadership is undergirded by a servant's heart and delegated authority is based on Christlike qualities. (To get more details on this subject go to Lessons 45-50 in my online discipleship school www.foundationpub.org.)

Servant leadership is of necessity much in the same way that our physical bodies need a skeleton. *New Testament leadership is established for the purpose of providing a framework for effective ministry among all the members of the body.*

> [2] "What I am arguing for is a balance between top-down and bottom-up ministry. There is always a need for order within the organism. Yet the purpose of the leadership structure is not to control ministry but to create structures and a climate where ministry is fostered throughout the life of the church community."

The Dark Ages were dark because the word of God was taken from the people while a false system of worship was instituted. [3] "The Reformation recovered the truth of the priesthood of all believers. But it failed to restore the necessary practices that embody this teaching...In the typical Protestant church, the doctrine of the priesthood of all believers is no more than a sterile truth."

Understanding the concept of the New Covenant priesthood should be a foundation for all believers. It is a foundation for understanding and living as a worshipful people. Actually, this understanding should be the foundation for all ministries.

God is seeking a people who will not only be redeemed from their sins but who will become His very dwelling place, His body, and His priests. In the book of I Peter 2:5 it shows us that we are:

> "Living stones, being built up into a spiritual house, a holy priesthood, to offer up spiritual sacrifices acceptable to God through Jesus Christ."

It is God's desire to take us beyond the point of just knowing about Him. He is at work in our hearts and His desire is it to LIVE IN US and WORK THROUGH OUR LIVES. Philippians 3:13 says, "for it is God who is at work in you, both to will and to work for His good pleasure." Then we see in Ephesians 2: 10 that,

"We are God's masterpiece. He has created us anew in Christ Jesus, so that we can do the good things He planned for us long ago." (New Living Translation)

The heart of God is that we would come to know Him in a very intimate way. However, our relationship with God has a practical side to it also. Worship has to do with our personal devotion and spiritual relationship with God, while good works are the practical outworking of this relationship with Him. This is not a calling for just a few elite people in the body of Christ, but it is the call of each Christian.

Each person in the body of Christ is a 'living stone' who is being built together with the other members into a spiritual house or dwelling place for God's Spirit. At the same time we are each also called to be 'priests' who offer up 'spiritual sacrifices'. The Spirit of God is calling each member of the body of Christ to become His very dwelling place, His body, and His priests.

THE DWELLING PLACE OF GOD

God has created man for fellowship and His ultimate goal is to have His dwelling place among men. To be the very place where God dwells is the ultimate calling of each of our lives as Christians. To be His dwelling place should be one of our main priorities in life.

The Tabernacle of Moses is a blueprint to teach spiritual truth from the Bible. A blueprint is a pattern that we can look to and learn how to do something. What we want to learn from the Tabernacle of Moses is a pattern for personal devotion or worship, which results in good works.

In the book of Exodus we see God bringing the children of Israel out of Egypt with mighty signs and wonders. After this mighty display of power they soon found themselves in a wilderness. It was here in the wilderness where Moses was commanded to build a Tabernacle for the Lord according to the pattern shown Him on Mt. Sinai where he received the Old Covenant Law (Exodus 19 through 30). The Tabernacle of Moses demonstrates the first step in establishing a dwelling place for God among men.

The Tabernacle of Moses was movable, or transient. This speaks of the fact that the Old Covenant, by which came the

Tabernacle of Moses, was temporary or transitory. The Law was not meant to be established as permanent, but to lead us to Christ and the New Covenant of the Spirit, which would be eternal. It was never God's desire to dwell in something that man made, but in man.

The Tabernacle of Moses where God dwelt temporarily was simply a blueprint pointing to the time of Christ. God finally took up His permanent dwelling place in 'the man Christ Jesus' so that He could transform man's heart into His dwelling place (Ephesians 1:13-14; I Corinthians 6:19).

If you look at **DIAGRAM A1** on this page you can see a picture of the outside of the Tabernacle of Moses.

> [4] "The Tabernacle of Moses was basically a tent and a courtyard with certain furnishings, designed by God and constructed by Moses as a dwelling place for the manifest presence of the Lord, that He might dwell among His people whom He had called out of captivity in Egypt. Now that we are under a New Covenant, why is the Tabernacle of Moses important today?"

Its importance is in the fact that through looking at the "Copy and Shadow" of the Tabernacle of Moses we can learn about the heavenly things of Christ (Hebrews 8:8:5). The law was to teach us and lead us to Christ. **Diagram A1**

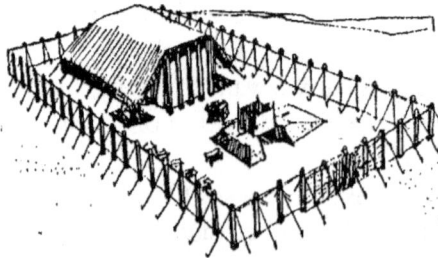

In John Chapter 2:13-22, when Jesus was cleansing the temple in Jerusalem and the Jews were arguing with Him, He declared to them that He was the new temple. God tabernacled among us in the man Jesus Christ and in Him dwelt the fullness of the Godhead bodily (Colossians 1:19; 2:9). Jesus is the Cornerstone of the church, the new temple and we as living stones have been laid on Him and are being built together with Him to be a dwelling place for the

Living God.

⁴ "The writers of the New Covenant continually refer to the Lord Jesus in the terminology of the Tabernacle, (High Priest, Lamb of God, etc.). Countless references are made to the Tabernacle to expound upon and explain the ministry of Jesus." It would have been interesting to hear exactly how Jesus taught the disciples on the road to Emmaus as he, "beginning with Moses and with all the prophets, explained to them the things concerning Himself in all the Scriptures" (Luke 22:27).

As New Covenant Christians we cannot forget the heritage of the Old Covenant Law. The Law was a prophecy that would be fulfilled. Jesus is the fulfillment of all that the Law, Psalms and Prophets taught (Luke 24:25-27). To get a full grasp of what the Bible teaches we need to see how the Old and New Covenants work together.

The apostle Paul showed us in I Corinthians 10:11 that all that happened to Israel was for our example and learning. There is a popular saying that goes, "The Old Covenant is the New concealed or hidden and the New Covenant is the Old revealed or made manifest."

Our journey as believers in Christ has much resemblance to the journey of the children of Israel. Just as they were brought out of Egypt by the blood of the lamb, we have been delivered from this present evil age through the blood of Jesus; however, that's not the end of our journey. After the crossing of the Red Sea and the destruction of Pharaoh's army, the children of Israel found themselves in a wilderness. It was here in the wilderness that they were commanded to build the Tabernacle of Moses and learn how to worship God.

As I discussed in my last book, we soon discover that following Jesus many times leads us into a wilderness of persecution, temptation and difficulties. It is through these circumstances that we must learn how to worship God. We can only overcome by worshipping God with our whole heart, obeying His word and allowing His Spirit to dwell within us. As we grow in the understanding that we are the dwelling place of God's Spirit, then we will be empowered to fulfill His purposes for our lives.

HOLY PRIEST IN AN UNGODLY AGE

The central person in the Old Covenant worship was the
High Priest. He was the most important person in the entire nation
because he represented Israel before God in offering sacrifices in the
Tabernacle of Moses where God dwelt among His people. God
chose Aaron and his sons to serve Him as priests. If you look at
Diagram A2 you can see a picture of the Aaronic High Priest.

Diagram A2

The Old Covenant priesthood was to be exclusively for
Aaron and his descendants. No one else was allowed to function in
the priestly office and the priestly office could only be entered by
family birthright (Exodus 28:1; 29:9; Numbers 4:3; Hebrews 5:4).
However, in all the beauty and glory of the Old Covenant High Priest
he was still just a blueprint, which pointed towards the Messiah yet to
come in human flesh.

The book of Hebrews is all about the contrast between the
Old and New Covenants. This book shows the superiority of the
New Covenant established by the death, burial and resurrection of
Jesus Christ. Hebrews 5:10 says that Jesus Christ was "designated by
God as a High Priest according to the order of Melchizedek."
Melchizedek is first mentioned in Genesis 14 in connection with
Abraham. The Hebrew word for Melchizedek is 'Malkiy-Tsedeq'
which means:

1) (#4428,4427 *STRONG'S)* 'KING ROYAL, TO REIGN,
TO ASCEND THE THRONE, TO INDUCT INTO
ROYALTY.'

2) (#6664, 6663 *STRONG'S)* 'TO RIGHT, EQUITY,

PROSPERITY JUSTICE, RIGHTEOUSNESS, CLEANSE, JUSTIFY.'

This word "Melchizedek" is found in Psalms 110:1-4; Hebrews 5:6, 10; 6:20; 7:1, 10, 11, 15, 17, 21. Thus the word is found two times in the Old Covenant and nine times in the New Covenant for a total of eleven times. The book of Hebrews provides the primary Scriptural basis for the study of Melchizedek.

On the basis of these scriptures we can see that Jesus is a High Priest after the order of Melchizedek. Let's take a look at the differences between the New Covenant High Priest Jesus and the Old Covenant High Priest Aaron.

The Aaronic priests were born by natural means, but Jesus was begotten by the power of the Holy Spirit born through the virgin birth (Luke 1:35) to become the Great High Priest. Hebrews 1:5 and 2:17 says:

"Thou Art My Son, Today I Have Begotten Thee"..."Therefore, it was necessary for Jesus to be in every respect like us, His brothers and sisters, so that He could be our merciful and faithful High Priest before God..." (N.L.T.; EMPHASIS MINE).

A priest is someone designated by God to stand between Himself, a Holy God, and a sinful people offering up sacrifices for the sins of the people. The Aaronic priests were ordained to offer up the sacrifices prescribed by the Law of Moses.

"For every High Priest is taken from among men is APPOINTED ON BEHALF OF MEN IN THINGS PERTAINING TO GOD, in order to offer both gifts and sacrifices for sins...according to the Law" Hebrews 5:1; 8:4 (EMPHASIS MINE)

These priests offered up to God the blood of goats and calves (Hebrews 9:12). However, there was a problem with the priest and the sacrifices under the Old Covenant. FIRST OF ALL, the Aaronic priests were only men. SECOND OF ALL, they were under a temporary sacrifice system until the fullness of times (Galatians 4:4). Yes, the Aaronic high priest was set apart for a holy service, but he like other

men needed daily to offer up sacrifices, FIRST FOR HIS OWN
SINS, and then for the sins of the people.

The Law appoints men as High Priests who are weak
(Hebrews 7:27-28). So we see that the Aaronic priests were mere
men and they were under a temporary system. The Law had a glory,
but it was fading in comparison to the coming time of the Messiah
(Hebrews 9:10). Chapter 10:1-4 of Hebrews shows us the weakness
of the 'sacrifice system' under the Old Covenant. The New Living
Translation says:

> "The old system in the law of Moses was only a shadow of the
> things to come, not the reality of the good things Christ has
> done for us. The sacrifices under the old system were repeated
> again and again, year after year, but they were never able to
> provide perfect cleansing, the sacrifices would have stopped,
> for the worshippers would have been purified once for all time,
> and their feelings of guilt would have disappeared. But just the
> opposite happened. Those yearly sacrifices reminded them of
> their sins year after year. For it is not possible for the blood of
> bulls and goats to take away sins."

The Law could only give a "knowledge of sin" (Romans 3:20)
and through the sacrifices of the Old Covenant, man could approach
a Holy God by faith in the blood that was shed which pointed to the
future Messiah (For more details refer to 'Building Your Spiritual
House' Section I, Lesson 5: Why The Law?). This provided a
temporary atonement but did not have the power to cleanse the inner
thoughts from sin.

God ordained the Old Covenant Law for a 'season' but it was
just a blueprint of the good things that were coming to mankind
through the New Covenant High Priest Jesus Christ. Paul describes
the coming of Christ as the 'fullness of times' (Gal. 4:4) when God
established a New Covenant with mankind through His own Son.
Christ stepped into time, not as a replacement of the Law but as the
very fulfillment of the entire Old Covenant predicted concerning the
Messiah.

It was in the fullness of times when the pre-existing Christ
took upon Himself human flesh (Phil. 2:6-7). John 1:14 says that,
"the Word became flesh, and dwelt or tabernacled among us, and we
beheld His glory, glory as of the only begotten from the Father, full

of grace and truth." He came into the world as Immanuel, which means 'GOD WITH US' (Matt. 1:23). Hebrews 2:14 says that because, "we are human beings — made of flesh and blood — Jesus also became flesh and blood by being born in human form" (N.L.T) to become our High Priest.

Unlike the Aaronic priest, Jesus as our Great High Priest did not enter into an earthly Tabernacle "made with hands, a mere copy of the true one, but into heaven itself, now to appear in the presence of God for us" (Hebrews 9:24). Jesus is the mediator of the New Covenant, which is established on better promises (Hebrews 8:6). Jesus unlike Aaron was holy, innocent, undefiled, unstained by sin and exalted above the heavens (Hebrews 7:26). The Old Covenant priests always had to offer sacrifices for their sins and the sins of the people, but Jesus offered up Himself ONCE AND FOR ALL. It is the ONE sacrifice of Christ that has dealt with the sin problem forever:

> "He, having offered one sacrifice for sins for all time, sat down at the right hand of God...And their sins and their lawless deeds I will remember no more. Now where there is forgiveness for these things, there is no longer any offering for sin." (Hebrews 10:12,17)

We also need to recognize that the Aaronic priesthood was limited to the nation of Israel, but JESUS CHRIST THE HIGH PRIEST AFTER THE ORDER OF MELCHIZEDEK HAS AN ETERNAL MINISTRY TO ALL NATIONS (Revelation 5:5-9). The ministry of Jesus is universal, ministering to all men without prejudice or partiality.

The ministry of Jesus as our High Priest is also an eternal ministry. Because of death, the Old Covenant priests were prevented from continuing, but JESUS, BECAUSE HE ABIDES FOREVER, HOLDS HIS PRIESTHOOD PERMANENTLY (Hebrews 7:23 - 24) seated forever on the throne of grace. This throne is not a big chair somewhere in outer space but is a symbolic picture of the supreme authority given to Christ through His resurrection from the dead. He entered Heaven to appear in the presence of God for us and as our High Priest He exercises every function of His office in endless life and power. This endless life and power never cease for a moment since it will never end, for He will never end.

Jesus came to bridge the gap between God and sinful man. Man needed someone to stand in the gap so he could get back to God. Jesus filled that gap as the perfect holy sacrifice for our sins. Now through His resurrection from the dead and ascension into heaven He ministers before God the Father as our merciful and faithful High Priest. It is because of Him that we can now enter into the very presence of God.

Created for Good Works

To be the very place where God dwells is our ultimate calling, and it is out of this relationship with Him that we do good works. Many people get confused between what the Bible calls DEAD WORKS and GOOD WORKS. Basically, a dead work is doing something so you can be seen as good, or doing religious or non- religious activity to try and gain God or man's approval. What makes it totally dead is that it has no eternal value in the eyes of the one and true God. They are works motivated by the desire to ease a guilty conscience, or promote self.

A 'dead work' will not help you get to God or receive His forgiveness and acceptance (For more detail refer to my online school of discipleship www.foundationpub.org Lesson 7: The 'Cycle of Dead Works'). Dead works are based on self. Self is living independent of God's ability and trusting in our own ability. Ephesians 2:19-20 says, "it is by grace that you are saved, through faith. This does not depend on anything you have achieved; it is the free gift of God; and because it is not earned no man can boast about it. For God has made us what we are, CREATED IN CHRIST JESUS TO DO THOSE GOOD DEEDS WHICH HE PLANNED FOR US TO DO" (Philippians Translation).

It is only by resting from our own dead works and entering into the grace of God that we can fulfill His plans for our lives. Good works are not motivated by self but motivated by the Holy Spirit. Good works are the result of having a relationship with God. They are not done to try and get to God or gain His approval but are the results of an obedient heart being directed by His Spirit. The good works of the New Covenant priest are not only offering up our spiritual sacrifices unto God, but also loving and serving others (Hebrews 13:16).

We have been brought into a holy priesthood and as priests we are called to stand between God and a sinful world. Just as Jesus came and partook of our humanity, when we were born again, we partook of His divine nature (I Peter 1:4) and are connected to his throne of grace. We have already seen that Jesus Christ is the word made flesh and through Him God dwelt among us. However, Jesus left this world and sent the Holy Spirit to be our Helper.

We are called to be representatives of Christ in this world. It is through our lives that the Risen Christ who not only lives in heaven interceding for us, but also lives in our hearts by His Spirit and touches others. When talking about faith James the apostle stresses the importance of our faith having a practical side. He says,

"Dear brothers and sisters, what's the use of saying you have faith if you don't prove it by your actions? That kind of faith can't save anyone. Suppose you see a brother or sister who needs food or clothing, and you say, 'Well, good-bye and God bless you; stay warm and eat well' — but then you don't give that person any food or clothing. What good does that do? So you see, it isn't enough just to have faith. FAITH THAT DOESN'T SHOW ITSELF BY GOOD DEEDS IS NO FAITH AT ALL — IT IS DEAD AND USELESS" James 2:14-17 (N.L.T. Emphasis Mine).

Works cannot give us salvation, but good works will help others. Our faith in Christ is demonstrated by what we do and when we don't reach out to others in love, our faith is dead and useless to this world.

To walk in the manifest presence of the Spirit and be light in the midst of a dark world is our calling. As priests we have been called to proclaim the virtues of Him who has called us out of darkness into His marvelous light (I Peter 2:9). We proclaim Christ's virtues in many ways: through our prayers, praise, worship, giving, relationships, marriages, godly conduct, mercy shown to others or simply obeying the governments of our land.

The Sacrifices of a Priest

When the word sacrifice is mentioned, what mental pictures go off in your mind? You could think of an athlete or maybe a Satanist. It might even be that you think of the hard work someone does at a job or the sacrifice of a mother for her child.

As I use the word sacrifice I want you to think of it as an offering. An offering is something we freely give. Jesus freely offered Himself upon the cross for our sins. I have already said that the Old Covenant sacrifices pointed towards the cross. However, the New Covenant also speaks about spiritual sacrifices that we as New Covenant priests should offer up to God. These sacrifices are not to add to the sacrifice of the cross, but are the result of a thankful heart, which has been given eternal life through the one well-pleasing sacrifice of Christ.

The Sacrifice of Our Bodies

God desires our worship and the beginning of our spiritual worship is the offering up of our bodies. Paul in Romans 12:1 says that part of our spiritual service of worship as priest is the offering of our bodies as living sacrifices. In this age we are constantly at war and have to learn to walk by faith in Christ.

At the core of this war lies the necessity to have our minds renewed in meditation on the truth of the gospel by the power of the Spirit. The primary tactic that the enemy uses is disinformation. The world, the flesh, and the devil work in cooperation to misinform, deceive, mislead, and misrepresent the people of God, and by all and every means subvert their worship.

The renewal of the mind leads to transformed actions governed by the Holy Spirit by which God is acceptably worshiped with our lives. Our bodies are to be the temple of the Holy Spirit, but if we do not present our bodies unto Him wholly then we will not be filled fully so that we can display His glory. (To get more details on this subject go to my online school of discipleship Lessons 23 and 24 The Sacrifice of our Bodies at www.foundationpub.org)

The Sacrifice of Praise

The book of Hebrews, which gives us, such a wonderful view of the Old and New Covenants points us to the superiority of Jesus Christ. According to the flesh Jesus was a descendant of King David who was of the tribe of Judah. The word for Judah means, "Praise" and David was one who praised God with his whole heart. The last chapter of Hebrews encourages us, based on the one sacrifice of Christ, to "continually offer up a sacrifice of praise to God, that is, the fruit of lips that give thanks to His name" (Hebrews 13:15-16).

In the same way that incense on the altar was to continually ascend up to God so He desires our hearts to continually speak, sing and shout His victorious praises. The best picture of praise in the Bible is David and Acts 15:16 says that that God has restored the "Tabernacle of David" in the New Covenant.

The 'Tabernacle of David' was the tent that he set up in Jerusalem (II Samuel 6:12-17). The 'Tabernacle of David' was an open tent with only the Ark of the Covenant under it. It is through the 'Tabernacle of David' that we learn the importance of praise and worship. The significance of the 'Tabernacle of David' is that they had priests who praised and worshiped God 24 hours a day (I Chronicles 16:37).

In Hebrews 13:15 it says that the sacrifice of praise is the fruit of lips that give thanks to His name. In looking at the word for 'give thanks' in the Greek it means to confess. Praise is simply making confessions of faith to the "Apostle and High Priest of our confession" (Hebrews 3:1).

Whether we have musical instruments or not we can still lift up our voices and begin to confess God's goodness, mercy, saving power, love towards us, etc. We can lift up shouts of triumph or just begin to sing of His grace reminding ourselves of what Christ did for us at the cross and what He can do for others and us right now.

Let the praises of God be in your heart and on your lips. Lift up the sacrifice of praise and let the power of God come into your life. When we begin to praise it is like opening up a window and allowing the wind of the Spirit to come into our hearts.

Paul the apostle encourages us to be filled with the Spirit and to "speak out to one another...offering praise with voices [and instruments]" (Eph. 5:19 Amplified). This is a place of great power as God manifests Himself to our hearts. (To get more details on this subject go to my online school of discipleship Lessons 25 and 26 The Sacrifice of Praise at www.foundationpub.org)

The Sacrifice of Prayer

"The sacrifice of the wicked is an abomination to the Lord, But the *prayer of the upright is His delight*" (Proverbs 15:8). God takes great pleasure when we pray to Him. In Revelation 5:8 we can see a heavenly viewpoint of prayer and it is seen as 'golden bowls full of incense.' Prayer is a sweet aroma that pleases God. This is a heart that is completely surrendered to Him and trusting that He will answer.

Prayer is fellowship and asking requests from our Heavenly Father. As a holy priesthood we are called to come boldly before the very throne of God for He takes delight in our spiritual sacrifices.

As a holy priesthood we are called to pray. I Thessalonians 5:17 tells us to 'pray without ceasing.' Keeping an attitude of prayer at all times is essential. In the 18th century the evangelist John Wesley said that God was limited to the prayers of the saints. God can do anything He wants, but He has chosen to use His body of priests to be His "House of Prayer" in the earth.

Jesus told us to pray and trust God for everything, from our daily bread to asking that the kingdom of God come on the earth (Matt. 6:9-11). Through prayer we become co-laborers with God. Praying is walking with God and allowing Him to walk in us and work His will through us. (To get more details on this subject go to my online school of discipleship Lessons 28 and 29 The Sacrifice of Prayer at www.foundationpub.org)

The Sacrifice of Giving

God so loved us that He gave. This is the basis of all giving. As we look to our 'Giving God' it is not hard to understand the reasons why we should give.

The world has made it sound like all the church wants is your money. Though there have been corrupt practices in the history and some current parts of the church, that doesn't make giving wrong.

Paul was quoting the very words of Jesus when he said in Acts 20:35 that, "It is more blessed to give than to receive". The world has no concept of this kingdom idea. Paul saw giving as a pleasing sacrifice unto God. In commenting about the financial gift that he received from the church in Philippi he said that it was, "a fragrant aroma, an acceptable sacrifice, well-pleasing to God" (Philippians 4:18b). As a holy priesthood giving is part of offering up our spiritual sacrifices to God.

When you present your sacrifice of giving to the Lord make it a time of worship. It is not just throwing your money away! Giving is a covenant commitment to God and it is planting seed that will bring forth a plentiful harvest either in this age or the age to come.

As we give, we must give in faith knowing that it is the will of God. God desires to bless us and for us to be a blessing. Let us offer up to God the spiritual sacrifice of our giving and see the hand of God move upon our finances, as we allow Him to be our financial partner. (To get more details on this subject go to my online school of discipleship Lessons 30 and 31 The Sacrifice of Giving at www.foundationpub.org)

Working Unto The Lord

When God created man and put him in the garden, He told him to cultivate and keep it (Genesis 2:15). Man was to find fulfillment, not in idleness, but in a life of rewarding labor in obedience to God. Christians are not called to be lazy but should set an example of honest and hard work. No matter what vocation the Lord has placed you in; He has placed you there to proclaim His kingdom. You are a representative of the Lord Jesus Christ and as a holy priest you should display His faithfulness.

To be faithful to work is to be faithful unto the Lord. God has created us to find fulfillment, to provide for our needs, and to minister to others through the avenue of work.

There are some today who think they can take the easy way out and live off the government, parents or friends. There are others who say they are living by faith and refuse to work, expecting God to pay their bills. Paul the apostle had to confront such people who thought they could live this way. He said in II Thess. 3:10 that, "if anyone will not work, neither let him eat." I am not speaking to those who are in situations where they are disabled and cannot work.

We need to understand that if we are self-employed or work for someone else that we work for God, not man. In Ephesians 6:5 it talks about slaves submitting to their masters. In Western society we no longer have slavery, but we do have those who are over us in the work field. We are to obey their rules, listen to their instructions, and work diligently for our money. This is to be done in the sincerity of our hearts as unto Christ (Ephesians 6:5-6). Not just when they are looking, because we are rendering our service as to the Lord, and not to men.

If we are managers, or have our own business, we should treat our employees with respect and honor (Eph. 6:9). We should not threaten our workers (Eph. 6:9). It should be our desire to treat our workers as Christ would treat them since *WORKER* and *MANAGER* are held accountable before God for how they work and treat others. (To get more details on this subject go to my online school of discipleship Lesson 32 Working Unto The Lord at www.foundationpub.org)

Priests are Faithful Stewards

In the book of I Samuel 2:31-35 God was rebuking Eli the High Priest for his unfaithful sons who polluted the priesthood. They abused their place of authority, were sexually immoral and were greedy. God brought judgment upon them for their excesses and rose up a faithful priest named Samuel. God expects us to be faithful priests over the calling of God on our lives, faithful to our relationships and faithful in our finances. In all areas of our lives God desires us to be faithful.

To be faithful is to demonstrate God's likeness. God is always faithful and can be trusted in all situations. His desire is to raise up a faithful priesthood that will display His faithfulness. As we walk in the manifest presence of the Lord we will live a life of faithfulness to God, our family, friends, etc, and this will demonstrate to the world that Jesus is our Lord. (To get more details on this subject go to my online school of discipleship Lesson 33 Stewardship at www.foundationpub.org)

Understanding Civil Authority

In a day when anarchy seems to be the rule, as Christians we need to understand the role of human governments. It is in Romans 13:1 where we can clearly see that God has ordained human governments as an extension of His rule.

We are told to obey the civil authority that we find ourselves subject to. The natural tendency we have is to take the easy way out and live any way we want to live. However, we are not an exception to the rule. There are laws to the city, province, state and country that you live in. We may be a holy priesthood serving in the kingdom of God, but we also live in this world and are subject to the civil laws of the land. Being obedient to the laws shows our obedience to God and serves as a witness for Christ.

Through Christ we have entered into the kingdom of God and have become a holy priesthood. However, until He returns as the 'King of kings' to bring this world completely under His subjection by force, we will be the citizens of a natural country. Some rulers and governments may be wicked, but we must pray for the rulers to change and obey the laws they have made, unless those laws cause us to disobey the word of God.

As a holy priesthood we should be model citizens to our neighbors, relatives and working partners. God has ordained the civil authority to set the laws and enforce them, but it is the Christians' duty to support that process with prayer and godly counsel.

We should not retreat to some cave thinking everything will take care of itself; instead, we need to be the salt that keeps civil authority being a blessing to the city and country it is serving as long as we are able to voice our opinions. As the last days come upon us there will be no political solutions to solve the problems the world will face. At that time due to persecution, we may have to retreat from the public square of politics, but we can never retreat from sharing the gospel of the kingdom. (To get more details on this subject go to my online school of discipleship Lesson 35 Civil Authority at www.foundationpub.org)

Merciful Priests

How do you respond when you see hurting people? Is your heart moved with compassion? Are you genuinely concerned about people? These are important questions because they reveal the attitudes of our heart. We are instructed in Colossians 3:12 to "put on a heart of compassion, kindness, humility, gentleness and forbearance towards others."

Jesus Christ is a merciful high priest who can have compassion upon our weaknesses (Hebrews 4:15). As His priests we need to demonstrate to this hurting world His mercy. Mercy will reach out, care, sympathize and help people. God has had mercy on us, and we need to have mercy on others.

As a holy priesthood living in the presence of our merciful God we need to show mercy to our hurting world. If as Christians, we don't reach out to be a blessing to this world then who will? We are not just called to offer up spiritual sacrifices but are also created to do good works that will be a benefit to others. Christians are to be the salt of the earth and salt is a preserving agent. Through being merciful, we bring preservation to that which is decaying in society. The gospel is the only remedy for the social ills that our society faces. (To get more details on this subject go to my online school of discipleship Lesson 37 A Life of Mercy at www.foundationpub.org)

A Pattern for Personal Devotion

In understanding our High Priest Jesus Christ, we come to realize that we are now a 'holy priesthood' that is born of His Spirit to offer up spiritual sacrifices which are acceptable to God (I Peter 2:5). We have entered this priesthood by divine birthright (John 1:12-13). It is our privilege and right to enter into the very presence of God through the One Sacrifice of Christ.

I want to go back to the blueprint of the Tabernacle of Moses to teach you how you can use this as a pattern for your personal devotion unto God. Just as the Tabernacle had to be made in a specific way, so the priest had to perform their service in a prescribed way, which was the pattern of worship for the priest under the Old Covenant.

If you look at **DIAGRAM A3** on the next page you will see the furniture that was used in the Tabernacle of Moses. It will also help you if you turn back to **DIAGRAM A1** so you can see a view of the Tabernacle from the outside. What I want to do now is walk you through the Tabernacle of Moses taking you to every piece of furniture. Under the Old Covenant the priest had to follow the prescribed order of worship in their daily service to God.

IMAGINE THAT YOU ARE WALKING THROUGH THIS WITH THE PRIEST BECAUSE YOU ARE A NEW COVENANT PRIEST. Allow this to develop in you an understanding of how to enter the manifest presence of God. It is God's desire to bring us into a more intimate relationship with Him where we live our lives in His very presence becoming His dwelling place. I am not laying down any law that you must follow, but I am presenting a pattern you can use when having your daily time of prayer and Bible study.

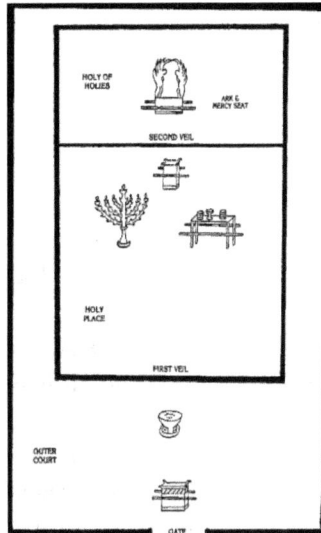

Diagram A3

First, the priest could not come to God empty handed. He had to have an offering to present to God. Under the Old Covenant there were five prescribed offerings. Each of these offerings has a symbolic significance of its own, but ultimately, they pointed to the one sacrifice of Christ. For the priest to enter into the tabernacle he first had to go to the Altar of Burnt Offering and offer up his sacrifice there.

The Altar of Burnt Offering was a very large grate almost like a barbecue. As a matter of fact, it was so big that all the other pieces of furniture together could fit into this one piece. This spoke of the all sufficiency of the Altar of the cross of Christ. There is no other way to enter into the presence of God without first accepting the One Sacrifice of Christ on the cross. Jesus said, "I am the way, and the truth and the life; no one comes to the Father, but through Me" (John 14:6).

We must first of all look to the all sufficiency of the blood of Jesus to cleanse us from all of our sins. There is no other way to enter into the presence of God except through the blood of the cross. We cannot approach God based on our works but based on our faith in the work of Christ for us.

After the priest offered up his sacrifices he then went to the Bronze Laver. Basically, this was like a big bathtub made out of solid bronze. The Aaronic priests were ordained and entered into service at the age of 30. When this happened, they had to come to this Bronze Laver and be baptized in it. This was a once and for all thing. Jesus was baptized at the age of 30 and when we received salvation we followed our Savior into the waters of baptism. However, as the priest's daily ministered in the Tabernacle they daily had to come to this Bronze Laver and clean themselves.

As we walk in this world ministering as a priest of God, we get dirty spiritually...we sin. Therefore, we need to be cleansed. We don't have to be reborn again or be baptized again; we only have to wash our hands and feet, which is a display our service to God and our walk with Him. The washing that we submit to is not natural water, but the living word of God. The Holy Spirit uses the Bible to wash us clean.

When we look into the Bible, it is like looking into a mirror. The Bible is God's holy looking glass that reveals our sin. [3] "At the same time, the Bible is also like a tub of hot water that the Holy Spirit uses to cleanse us, as we allow Him to. The Holy Spirit scrubs us down really good where we're dirty with the Word of God."

It is here at the Bronze Laver where we look at the reflection of the word of God and allow it to renew our minds; reminding ourselves of the great promises God has given us in Christ (Romans 12:2). As we allow the power of God's word to renew us we will be strengthened to fulfill our duties as God's priests.

Next, the priest enters into the tabernacle itself. There were two sections to the Tabernacle of Moses. As the priest opens up the first curtain he enters into the Holy Place. No outside light is allowed here, but only the Gold Lampstand lights it up. Daily the priest had to fill this Gold Lampstand or Candlestick with the proper oil so the Holy Place would have light.

When Jesus Christ rose from the dead and ascended to the throne of God, He sent His Holy Spirit to those who would believe. As priests before our God, we must be filled with His Spirit daily. The Holy Spirit is our power source. Romans 8:14 says we are to be governed by the Holy Spirit. He is the One who illuminates our hearts to walk in the way of the Lord; therefore, we must continually be filled with the Spirit (Ephesians 5:18).

As the priest turned around, directly across the Holy Place was the Table of Shewbread. On this table there were 12 loaves of bread and daily the priest had to take the old bread out and put 12 new loaves on the table. This bread was called the 'bread of presence' because it sat before the presence of the Lord.

The priests were allowed to eat the old 'bread of presence' as they replaced it with new. In John 6:35 Jesus said, "I am the bread of life". The New Covenant meal for the New Covenant priesthood is the flesh and blood of Jesus Christ (John 6:53-57). As priests we must daily acknowledge the blood and body of Christ as our very life. Paul said, "it is no longer I who live, but Christ lives in me" (Galatians 2:20). It is here where we say, "not my will but thy will be done, I surrender all to you Lord!"

The priest has now come to the Altar of Incense and is right in front of the curtain, which leads into the second room of the Tabernacle, the Most Holy Place. Here at the Altar of Incense the priest takes the incense that has been crushed and blended together as a perfume of a sweet-smelling aroma. Upon this altar the priest lays the incense, and it goes up into the very presence of God.

As a holy priesthood we are to offer up spiritual sacrifices that are acceptable to Him. The incense that we offer up to Him is prayer and praise. This incense of our hearts lifted up in worship is well pleasing to Him.

Behind the second curtain or veil was the Most Holy Place or as it sometimes was called the Holy of Holies. This is where the Ark of the Covenant was, which represents the manifest presence of God. The High Priest alone entered this place only once a year (Hebrews 9:7). However, Jesus entered into the heavenly Holy Place and calls us as His New Covenant priests to come in with Him:

"Therefore, brethren, since we have full freedom and confidence to enter into the Holy of Holies [by the power and virtue] in the blood of Jesus. By this fresh new and living way which He initiated and dedicated and opened for us through the separating curtain (veil of the Holy of Holies), that is, through His flesh, And since we have [such] a great and wonderful and noble Priest [Who rules] over the house of God, Let us all come forward and draw near with true honest and sincere hearts in unqualified assurance and absolute conviction produced by faith...having our hearts sprinkled and purified from a guilty (evil) conscience and our bodies cleansed with pure water." (Hebrews 10:19-22 Amplified Bible)

His blood has given us a direct access unto the Father

(Ephesians 2:18). The veil has been torn and we are called in to enter his rest. Jesus is already seated and is perfected. He has entered His rest (Hebrews 3-4). He is calling us through the gospel of His free grace to lay everything aside and draw near to Him. Let the cry of our hearts be that we might know Him. Not just knowing facts about Him but having an intimate relationship with Him. God has a purpose for each one of our lives as His priests, however it is only through knowing Him that we can fulfill that purpose.

Chapter 5

FAITHFUL WORSHIPPERS TO THE END

"And I saw the woman drunk with the blood of the saints, and
with the blood of the witnesses of Jesus."
~Revelation 17:6~

The end of the age is going to be a time of unprecedented
trouble and religious confusion in advance to the final consummation
of the age. In the second chapter of this book we looked at what
I would describe as the spirit of Commercial Babylon. Although it
seems that the main aspect of Babylon is commerce, I do think there
is credence to say that there is also a religious aspect to Babylon in
Revelation 17-18.

Religious Babylon is not one grand organization in the same
way that the true church is not one physical organization, but it will
be a mixture of confused religion opposing the true covenant faith of
Christ among the nations. The final battle for the soul of man is the
Antichrist kingdom which will only last for a short period of time and
will be one organized attempt to subject humanity to open worship
of the beast, or the *man of lawlessness* which is how Paul describes him
in II Thessalonians 2:1-12.

The Protestant Reformers in the 1500's saw the Catholic
Church as Babylon. Others today see the World Council of
Churches or the Ecumenical movement of all religions joining with a
false Christian church as Babylon. Some say that this apostate
Christianity will be merged with Islam. Still others see the resurgence
of paganism manifested through the New Age being a titular head
for all religious faiths. Babylon is simply apostate humanity,

both secular and religious in opposition to Christ and His body.

Religious Babylon is embodied when apostate religious and political entities join together as an organized system to persecute the saints. Babylon was embodied in the Roman State. It also manifested itself in the Jewish authorities by persecuting the apostles and saints seen in the book of Acts. However, history and current trends demonstrate that Babylon has operated throughout history, for instance, during the Inquisitions of Europe, the persecution of the Protestant Reformers, and Hitler's regime, to name a few instances.

It was Karl Marx who said, "Religion is the opiate of the masses". Religious Babylon is that opiate of which Karl Marx spoke. In the same way that Commercial Babylon seduces the nations with covetousness, so Religious Babylon is being used to seduce multitudes of nations and tongues with the opiate of religion.

The seduction is in the form of a veil of religious confusion keeping people from the simple truth of the good news. Babylon can also be seen as a merger of the nation-state with religion or state worship, which you could call religious nationalism. It is in Matthew's gospel, that we find the clearest revelation concerning events, which will signal the return of Christ to the earth. In Jesus' response to the question posed by his disciples concerning His return and the end of the age, He says as quoted in the book of Matthew 24: 9 that: Vs 9b "You will be hated by all nations for My name's sake."

In looking at recent history, the two superpowers Russia formerly the Soviet Union and the United States opposed each other throughout the Cold War and everyone was terrified that at any time we could be wiped out by a nuclear exchange of weapons. At the falling of the Berlin Wall in 1992, everyone proclaimed peace and safety in the world as the Bear was declared and the Soviet Union collapsed. However, this could not have been further from the truth. Samuel P. Huntington in his book "The Clash Of Civilizations And The Remaking Of World Order" clearly defines the present state of world affairs.

The Cold War brought an identity crisis to many nations and they are now attempting to answer the most basic questions humans can face: **Who are we?**

[1] "And they are answering that question in the traditional way

human beings have answered it, by reference to the things that mean most to them. People define themselves in terms of ancestry, religion, language, history, values, customs and institutions. They identify with cultural groups: tribes, ethnic groups, religious communities..."

We have seen a more integrated economic system emerging in the world; however, the world is not leaning towards a singular religion. Sociologists have identified that since the fall of the Soviet Union, the world has become more religious, not less. Religions are one of the main motivating factors behind the conflict of nation rising against nation of which Jesus spoke. In addition to the conflict among nation-states, we are also seeing a growing rise of religious nationalism with the result of the true church being persecuted worldwide.

Drunk on the Blood of the Saints

Jesus said that the end of the age is going to be a time of great harvest. The Spirit of God is moving over the face of the earth, and multitudes are coming to a personal faith in Christ. The church has been planted among the nations and indigenous workers are taking their place and many times at their own peril. According to the U.S. Center for World Missions statistics in 2008, based on the rate compiled over the last 10 years, every day it is estimated 140,000 souls are brought into the kingdom of God worldwide. The vast majority of these new believers are in Asia, Africa and in South America.

Unlike in America, the place of leadership among the body of Christ comes at a cost in many nations. Outside of Western Nations, the church is experiencing exponential growth and open political, economic, and even physical persecution. Babylon in the book of Revelation is seen as being intoxicated on the blood of the saints. If Babylon cannot seduce you with its covetous spirit so that you partake of her nature, then she will try to wear you out with persecution and deception. I want to give you some current data on what the church among the nations is experiencing in regard to persecution.

I would think that most people are aware of the rise of persecution against Christians in Islamic countries. Islam merges its faith with its politics and the result is a state-run religion. All Islamic states have some form of persecution against believers, and it means death for many all over the world. The Muslim nations encompass approximately 1.2 billion people with nations in Africa, Asia, South Pacific and the Middle East.

India is one of the most populace nations on earth with an estimated 1.17 billion people. India has a growing church, but the believers of India are experiencing ardent persecution in recent years from Hindu Nationalists among some of its Provinces. Michelle A. Vue a journalist for the Christian Post writes. [2] "The violence against Christians is not the random work of a few break- away gangs. There is a close-knit network of Hindu fundamentalist organizations...which promotes the ideal of a national state for Hindus.

At least 60 Christians have been killed - although some Indian leaders say hundreds have died - and some 18,000 have been wounded. More than 250 churches have been razed or destroyed, 5,031 Christian homes have been burned down, and more than 50,000 Christians have been displaced in the Province of Orissa alone since August of 2008." I am not even mentioning the economic and social control the government in certain Provinces in India administers to those who identify with Christ. Yes this is happening in some provinces while great advances for the kingdom are being made in other areas of the country.

In Sri Lanka, Buddhist Nationalists are persecuting the followers of Christ. In June of 2008 the Buddhist Sinhala Nationalist Party was associated with a new wave of attacks on Christian pastors and churches sweeping Sri Lanka.

The nation of Russia only has a population of about 150 million people, but through their economic and religious influence from the Russian Orthodox Church they are able to influence many peoples. At the falling of the Soviet Union, the nation of Russia had an open door policy to religious faiths. Putin the leader of Russia has popularized a new Russia. The new Russia is one with the Russian Orthodox Church at its center. In a Time Magazine article titled, [3] "Putin's Reunited Russian Church" the author states, "Nationalism, based on the Orthodox faith, has been emerging as the Putin regime's major ideological resource.

The Church's assertiveness and presence is growing with little separation from the state. With a reunited Russian Orthodox Church,

Putin is pushing Russia's dominance in the global Orthodox movement. The Orthodox communion includes churches in Greece, Cyprus, Ukraine, Belarus and various Balkan states as well as Georgia, Armenia and Moldova."

According to an article written in the New York Times, a Russian Orthodox priest, who is a confidant of one region's most powerful politicians, gave a sermon that was repeated every few hours. His theme: Protestant heretics. [4] "We deplore those who are led astray: those Baptists, Evangelicals, Pentecostals and many others who cut Christ's robes like bandits, who are like the soldiers who crucified Christ, who ripped apart Christ's holy coat," declared the priest. Russian authorities are shutting down churches with new restrictive laws and making it difficult for those who are not government approved to operate openly.

China has a population of nearly 1.3 billion people. They have no official state religion but do promote a Confucian value system among Asian states, of which they are the most dominant. The Chinese government promotes a form of Han Nationalism, which is the most dominant ethnic group. The Han nationalists suppress the [5]"linguistic, regional, and economic difference among the Chinese population...It also provides a basis for the regime's opposition to Christianity, Christian organizations, and Christian evangelism."

China has the fastest house church growth in the world. [5]"Persecution against Christians varies from harassment, humiliation, fines and church closures to imprisonment, torture and forced labor. When Christians are arrested they are often beaten, at times leaving them with serious injuries and in need of hospital treatment". China does have Christian churches that are state recognized, but they are restricted and monitored by the government.

The reason I have mentioned some of the events happening around the world is because it is important that we see that the words of Christ are maturing or being more fully fulfilled. The gospel is going to all nations with great success and Religious Babylon, which is the merging of politics and religion, thrives on confusing and resisting the saints.

What is happening in the Western nations of the world where there is a long history of the Christian faith? Specifically, since the 1960's, Western nations have been going through what has been defined as a 'Culture War.' At the center of this war has been the issue of the Christian faith and its place in Western nations. The ideas are not anti-religious, but they are antichrist when it comes to the fundamentals of our faith. You can be a Christian as long as you take Christ out of your faith. To declare that Jesus Christ is the only means of salvation and publicly declare that is anathema in Babylon.

As I have already stated, secularism is not anti-religious since religious pluralism is accepted, but it is anti-Christian since those who take the word of God as the final truth are excluded or marginalized in the public square by ridicule. It is *the Babylonian idea that Christ is not God, but simply one of the many gods of the nations* who is worthy of worship. Secular humanism is not just a philosophical idea, but it is actually the religion of man-worship, and the end result is totalitarianism or state worship where the Emperor is god.

England has had hate crimes legislation for about 10 years, and they are ahead of the game. In 2009 Dale Hurd a CBN reporter has documented the shift in Britain. He reported that in Britain [6] "Doctors, nurses, adoptive parents, are deemed unfit because of their Christian beliefs. Christians are told not to speak about God in the workplace or they could be punished for offending homosexuals or Muslims."

A nation has never existed like America, nor do I believe one will ever exist like us again. Over the last 50 to 75 years, we have been the world's greatest economic power with the rest of the world in awe of our dominance and standard of living. At the same time, we have sent more missionaries around the world; have sent Christian television around the world, put out more Bibles and Christian books than you can keep count. The results have been much good, but the casual observer can know that as a whole our efforts have been mixed and many times what the world sees coming out of America is confusing.

America has had the greatest religious freedoms ever known in any nation. However, it seems that the tide is turning. Hate crimes legislation seems to be innocuous and harmless since we are protecting minorities. However, in the same way that European nations are singling out Bible believing Christians, so it seems that the American government is moving in the same direction. Hopefully we see this trend reversed. We can see that Transnational Corporations based in America have already embraced the Babylonian philosophy of no moral standards with strong policies advocating these same positions influencing Europe and Canada. It seems that the U.S.

government is moving in the same direction. The question is how do we respond as believers?

The main pathway that culture is trying to fundamentally change our faith is in the area of our sexuality. At the very core of Western social change has been the "Sexual Revolution" which has revolutionized our thinking on a whole array of moral issues, which goes to the very issue of worship. The enemy of our souls knows that sexual sin is an especially grievous sin to the heart of God. The reason is because "there's more to sex than mere skin on skin. Sex is as much spiritual mystery as physical fact. As written in Scripture, 'The two become one.'" (I Corinthians 6:16: The Message Translation). Illicit sexual activity is a gateway to greater darkness.

Understanding the covenant between husband and wife is a foundation for understanding the covenant between Christ and the church. If you don't understand the New Covenant, then you don't understand true worship and will be given to idolatry. In Ephesians 5:30-31, Paul reveals a mystery to us. It is an understanding of covenant, communion and oneness found only in the cross.

The New Testament only talks about two covenants. The secondary covenant of marriage simply comes from the original. The central covenant in the Old and New Testament is the blood covenant. The covenant between husband and wife originates out of the covenant of the cross of Christ, which we define as marriage.

The covenant is consummated when they are joined as one flesh through blood during sexual relations. A virgin bleeds when her hymen is broken and within the seed or semen is blood, which is the transmitting of life. *The shedding of blood is a bond of life.* Unlike our covenant with Christ, marriage is not an eternal covenant, but it is nonetheless a covenant supposed to be adhered to as long as the couple remains alive. I am not even going to get into the issue of *divorce and remarriage for the believer* since it would be a book in itself and others have already adequately addressed the subject.

I will say that when you understand covenant your view of marriage will become biblically based. Although I am not addressing divorce and remarriage in this book, I understand that we live in a fallen world with many intricacies complicating relationships. We should not lower our standards based on cultural difficulties, but I don't think we should judge another until we have walked in their shoes. Each situation is unique, and we can't make blanket statements, which affect people's actual lives. The Bible does allow for divorce and remarriage, but *the church is supposed to be an example of covenant relationship* of which marriage is the main focus.

The marriage comes out of the very heart of God and it defines sexual relations. According to the Bible, outside of the covenant of marriage, all sexual relations are under the wrath of God. The word *fornication is used many times to describe sexual sin in the New Testament*, and it includes adultery, homosexuality, bestiality, pornography or any other sexual deviance.

In the same chapter, which Paul spoke of the mystery of marriage he said, "For this you know, that no fornicator, unclean person, nor covetous man, who is an idolater, has any inheritance in the kingdom of Christ and God. Let no one deceive you with empty words, for because of these things the wrath of God comes upon the sons of disobedience" (Ephesians 5:5-6).

We all must come to terms with our sexuality and deal with areas in our hearts that yield to ways contrary to God's kingdom. If we will learn to yield our hearts completely to the kingdom then the Spirit will give us the power to live godly lives in the midst of a society given to sexual activity opposed to God's kingdom (Study Lesson 10: A Lifestyle of Repentance at www.foundationpub.org to understand temptation and overcoming the flesh ruled life).

It is interesting to look at the purpose for which God brought such devastating judgment on the inhabitants of the land of Canaan through the children of Israel. If you look at Leviticus 18 just after the children of Israel were instructed against various sexual sins, it warns them that by following the former inhabitants' sexual ways that they would be judged. It describes the sexual acts as actually defiling the land and tells them that if they give themselves to such degradation, the land would actually vomit them out, describing a thorough judgment.

As the end of the age approaches, we will see increased lawlessness or unrestrained sin (Matt. 24:12). The impurity or uncleanness of sexual sin is one of the primary ways that lawlessness gets a grip on a person's heart, leading to further lawlessness. We can look at modern society and see that it has given itself over to sexual sin while purity is actually mocked. Sexual sin is a gateway where your moral compass becomes distorted which ends in idolatrous worship.

A George Barna survey in 2008 indicated that in America only one-third of all adults (34%) believe that moral truth is absolute and unaffected by the circumstances. Europe is way ahead of America in its moral decline regarding the absolutes of moral truth. In the U.S. slightly less than half of the born-again adults (46%) believe in absolute moral truth. *Lawlessness is the rejection of moral absolutes.* It is the idea that sexual sin depends on the circumstances, which is *the idolatry of relativism.*

The issue with sexual sin is not what the world does, but what we do as believers. One of the main issues of our time surrounding sexuality and society is homosexuality. I have worked side by side with homosexuals and I don't judge nor treat them differently than anyone else in the workplace. Paul said that we are not to judge those outside of the church, but those who call themselves believers (I Corinthians 5:9-13).

In the church, we need to help restore people caught in the sin of adultery, fornication, pornography, homosexuality or any sexual sin. It is the spiritually mature (Galatians 6) who will be able to restore struggling and fallen believers since they understand the grace of God. Mature believers understand that it is only by abiding in the grace of God or we too could be overcome with corruption.

The church must never be afraid to call sin 'sin'. Yes, mercy triumphs over judgment. I like what the book of Jude says, "have mercy on some, who are doubting; save others, snatching them out of the fire; and on some have mercy with fear, hating even the garment polluted by the flesh" (Jude 1:22-23).

At the same time, we must teach the bride of Christ to live by the standards of God's word with no compromise. I know it is not a popular teaching, but the elders, or you may call them pastors, are actually supposed to restore, correct and in some extreme cases exclude church members who practice sinful lifestyles for the protection and sanctity of the life of fellowship among believers (Matt. 18:15-20; I Cor. 5:1-13).

Wisdom is the key to know how to relate with the world so that we can win them to Christ through loving them as God loves them (Colossians 4:2-6); while at the same time the wisdom to keep the bride pure from defilement. We are not called to throw stones at homosexuals or those caught in a myriad of sexual sins, but we are called with the power of the Spirit and mercy of God to heal the broken hearted. It is important that we address these issues, which are going to continue to confront us with the wisdom and power of Christ. Colossians 4:5 tell us to "conduct yourselves with wisdom toward outsiders, making the most of the opportunity." We must always remember that we are called to be salt to those entangled in sexual sin and salt is a preserving agent.

Apostasy and the End of the Age

To water down the faith like we have done in the West has the danger of making Christ in our image. We no longer teach the radical idea of covenant, but that we just need to accept Christ. A.W. Tozer addressed this subject years ago by saying:

> "The trouble is the whole 'Accept Christ' attitude is likely to be wrong. It shows Christ applying to us rather than us to Him. It makes Him stand hat-in-hand awaiting our verdict on Him, instead of our kneeling with troubled hearts awaiting His verdict on us. It may even permit us to accept Christ by an impulse of mind or emotions, painlessly, at no loss to our ego and no inconvenience to our usual way of life."

The word of the cross must be central to our message (To get further details on this subject read chapter 2 of "Running The Race To Win" order at www.FoundationPub.org).

You may not realize it but homosexual theology is gaining ground in parts of the church. I am amazed at how many people are falling for the twisted biblical interpretations concerning sexual relations. In 2009 the 4.7 million members of the Evangelical Lutheran Church are now allowing Gays and Lesbians to be ministers in their congregations. This is not to mention the 2 million members of the United Churches of Christ, 2.1 million members of the Episcopal Church USA, the Metropolitan Community Churches and many others who are embracing this deception.

The reason so many people have come to these conclusions is nothing short of apostasy. It is the same thing that happened in Israel when they chased after idols and gave themselves to sexual degradation. In a 2009 survey George Barna identifies 66% of Americans as Casual Christians.

A causal form of Christianity has gripped portions of the church in Western nations. It is what Paul called those who have "a form of godliness" but no transforming power; therefore, they have exchanged the lie for a truth. George Barna describes such people as driven by a desire for a pleasant and peaceful existence.

It is the same reason that Israel chased after other gods; so that they could live in a pleasant, prosperous and peaceful existence with its neighbors, but the end was always slavery to Babylon and judgment. It could be why there is a rise in the number of people who say they are Christians but hold to the doctrine of Universalism or some call it 'Ultimate Reconciliation'. It is the *idol of pluralism* where we synchronize our faith with all others.

Universalism basically says that all will be saved no matter what degradation you practice, and it does not matter if you worship Mohammed, Buddha or Christ you will be saved. Peter warned us that we would see such teachings in the last days.

"Vs. 18 For speaking out arrogant words of vanity they entice by fleshly desires, by sensuality, those who barely escape from the ones who live in error. Vs. 19 promising them freedom while they themselves are slaves of corruption; for by what a man is overcome, by this he is enslaved. Vs. 20 For if after they have escaped the defilements of the world by the knowledge of the Lord and Savior Jesus Christ, they again entangled in them and are overcome, the last state has become worse for them than the first. (II Peter 2:18-20)

In Romans Chapter 1:18-32, too many focus on homosexuality, which the chapter surely mentions the conduct, but the subject of the chapter is about worship or more accurately false worship and its consequences.

The book of Romans is called the gospel of God's grace. In Romans 1:16-17, Paul stated his theme: the good news of salvation, for all nations. In addition, to the good news, this text tells us that God is constantly speaking to men and women through the creation, and directly in their own hearts.

We see that instead of acknowledging the God of creation, men and women have exchanged the creation to become a god. Can anyone say, the 'Environmental Movement?' It has much more to do with worship than global warming. We need to be good stewards of the planet, but the current movement is many times not about simple stewardship, but borders on *earth idolatry*, which is *pantheism*.

The error described in Romans 1:18 is not the neglect of worship, but the **exchange** of worship. Man was created to worship God; therefore, within man's heart is an innate need to worship. If the void in man's heart is not filled with the Spirit of life, then he will exchange the truth for religion, immorality, covetousness, sports, entertainment etc. which is idolatrous worship. When culture exchanges true worship for false worship then there begins to be assembled, an organized attempt to suppress the truth, which results in various types of false worship systems.

Satan understands that at the core of man's innate need for worship is his sexuality identity. Creation expresses and declares that sexual union is between a man and woman. It was God's original intent and it is the crown of the creation story. To reject creations order is to reject the God of creation (Genesis 2:21-25).

When man reduces himself as nothing more than a part of the created order instead of created in the image of God then he identifies with the created order. The result is man's mind becoming corrupted with idolatry and therefore he brings himself under the wrath of God. [7]"Human unrighteousness most fundamentally consists in a refusal to worship God and a desire to worship that which is in the created order. Unrighteousness involves the refusal to give God his proper sovereignty in one's life."

God's love could not be just and holy if he did not exercise wrath against evil. The Father has reached out to us through the Son of God, but *if we reject the blood covenant, there is judgment* (Hebrews 10:26-31). God's wrath is not directed at homosexuality, but it is directed at idolatry, which is manifested in men and women rejecting God. This is spoken of as something that lies in the future which will be fully manifested at the end of the age (Romans 2:5, 8; 5:9; I Thess. 1:10). However, the reality is that God's wrath is revealed right now in giving people over to the darkness of their own hearts and demonic powers when they refuse to worship God.

[7] "By the worship of idols, human beings compound their enslavement to powers of darkness, who stand behind and energize all idolatrous action. In all of this they meet God's wrath…Idolatry destroys human dignity and freedom, and it ushers people directly into the experience of the wrath of God, whom they are seeking to reject."

If you look at the book of Revelation, a time is coming when God will openly judge sin. His wrath will be poured out in an evident way against those who give themselves to idolatry by rejecting the cross. We must be those bondservants who have yielded to the cross through our lives dedicated to the blood covenant. Just as the children of Israel were set apart by the power of God and the blood during the judgment of Egypt those dedicated to Him will be protected from the judgment and wrath of God.

Harvest: Salvation and Apostasy

Jesus talked about harvest and the end of the age. We are seeing a great harvest of souls happening worldwide among the nations of the earth. We will continue to see this harvest of souls as we witness the greatest outpouring of the Spirit this earth has ever seen prior to Christ return.

Israel had three main feasts yearly in which they were to come before the Lord and worship at the temple in Jerusalem (Deuteronomy 16:1-17). The three main feasts are 'the feast of Passover', 'the feast of Pentecost' and 'the feast of Tabernacles or Ingathering' which are fulfilled in the body of Christ. Jesus has become our 'Passover' (I Cor. 5:7-8), which we celebrate through our covenant meal, and the church has experienced an initial outpouring of the Spirit and first fruits of soul's called the 'feast of Pentecost' or the 'feast of First Fruits' beginning in Acts 2.

The end of the age is going to be preceded by a final outpouring of the Spirit and ingathering of souls pictured through the third feast that Israel was told to keep during the end of the year harvest, which is the 'feast of Ingathering' (Some see the millennial age as the ultimate fulfillment of the 'feast of Ingathering' or also called 'Tabernacles').

At the same time the church is experiencing a harvest of souls coming into the kingdom we are going to witness an antithesis of apostasy or falling away. *Salvation and apostasy will be happening simultaneously!* The end of the age is going to be a time of judgment on the threshing floor, which means it will be a time of great sifting and separation. The wheat and the tares will be separated.

The preterist theologian David Chilton says, "The apostasy happened in the first century. We therefore have no biblical warrant to expect increasing apostasy as history progresses; instead, we should expect the increasing Christianization of the world." A majority of historicists interpret the apostasy spoken of in II Thess. 2:3 as already past having happened during the Dark Ages. I agree that it was a great time of darkness when the word of God was taken from the people and apostasy prevailed. The Catholic Church systematically controlled nations and people through adulterating the truth, but it was *not the ultimate fulfillment*.

Jesus specifically talked about false prophets and false Christ's promoting myriads of deceptions before His return. The apostasy of the end of the age is not going to be one organized scheme, but complete confusion. Previously in chapter 2 of this book I said that the Hebrew's defined Babylon as mixed up or confused. As we progress towards the end of the age we are going to see this *'confused mixture'* grow like tares in the field of religion, politics, finance and social structures.

The confusion of the end of the age is the breaking down of absolutes into subjective grays producing a corrosive eroding to the foundations of faith, family and civil society. You can look at this erosion and instability as a precursor to the final dictatorial worship of the beast or more popularly termed the Antichrist. It is the breaking down of man's will so that he will not be able to resist the beast's powerful influence.

In this chapter I am specifically dealing with the *'confused mixture'*, which erodes the foundations of our faith. It is the breaking down of any soundness of truth into distortions, extreme ideas on both sides of the spectrum and outright deception. Paul said that a "time will come when they will not endure sound doctrine; but wanting to have their ears tickled, they will accumulate for themselves teachers in accordance to their own desires; and will turn away their ears from the truth and will turn aside to myths" (II Tim. 4:3-4). The confusion comes in the form of leading people away from the simple truth of our foundation: Christ Himself and the cross He told us we must embrace.

A recent example of this departing from the faith or *leaving sound doctrine* is when in 2010 a prominent leader in the body of Christ announced to his congregation that he has been a homosexual for 30 years. The end result is mixed up and confused people concerning the message of Christ. I see the doctrine of 'Universalism or Ultimate Reconciliation' as fueling the fire of this departure from the faith. The basic premise of this teaching is that there is neither hell nor any eternal punishment since Christ is going to reconcile all things to Himself. This reconciliation includes unbelievers, those of all religious faiths and those living in open unrepentant sin, since there really is no sin…Christ will reconcile 'all things'. One prominent author promoting these positions has labeled his message the 'doctrine of inclusion'. *It is taking a truth out of proportion to the whole body of scripture with the end result being apostasy.* It's embracing the *idols of materialism, relativism and pluralism.*

If you are a new believer, it does not take long to look at the church and listen to the many different teachers and become confused really quick. Instead of being established on the foundation of Christ, far too many people are established on ministry figures, which are gifted men. We need to receive the gift, but the reality is that they are still men and the arm of flesh will always fail. A minister is a servant gift, given to the body that is part of the family. I am not saying we don't need congregational and national leaders whom we respect and bring clarity to needed issues, but I am saying that we are never to idolize any ministry. I hope that we have learned the lesson by now that *no one is too big to fail!*

No one has a corner on truth. We just have a piece of a bigger picture. *I only 'know in part' and to see clearly I have to listen to others in the body of Christ to get a full picture of the word of God.* The part I have been given to emphasize is foundational. I am convinced that for us to grow spiritually, we need to be grounded in the foundational truth of the word of God. It is important that believers are equipped in at least a basic understanding of Christ our Messiah and the Spirit who has been sent to lead us into all truth (I John 2:20- 24).

The Berean's (Acts 17:11) were commended for searching the scriptures to make sure that what they were being taught was the truth and Paul the apostle who wrote large portions of the New Testament was the one teaching! Paul was not afraid to be challenged because he was firmly rooted and secure. At the same time, we should be able to defend our faith or be able to constructively explain what we believe. If it is the truth, it will stand up under scrutiny.

Defenders of the Faith

The Christian faith has been established for the last 2,000 years and Satan has tried with every wind of doctrine to blow it away from its original foundation. The main weapons of the enemy are enticing philosophies with a scriptural foundation that have been taken out of context.

Satan's first assault against mankind was when he deceived Eve in the Garden of Eden by twisting what God had originally said, which caused her to doubt and be confused about God's word (Gen. 3:7). Satan's main weapon against mankind and the church continues to be deception.

In I Timothy 4:1 Paul the apostle said that, "some will fall away from the faith," or you might say they will be blinded from seeing and understanding the truth by "paying attention to deceitful spirits and doctrines of demons". In this verse it is quite obvious that the words 'spirits and demons' are in the plural and not the singular. It is not often Satan personally who is the one blinding the minds of people, but the blinding comes from false doctrines, concepts, ideas, philosophies and teachings inspired by evil spirits. This is why the Bible warns the believer in I John 4:1, to "believe not every spirit, but try the spirits whether they are of God."

You see, the spirit of error is *truth* that has been taken out of *proportion* to the *whole body of truth*. We cannot build our faith or teachings on just one portion of the Bible, or we will fall into error. This is why Paul told Timothy in II Timothy 2:15 to "be diligent to present yourself approved to God as a workman who does not need to be ashamed, *handling accurately* the word of truth" (Emphasis Mine).

In the church of today we are always hearing some new revelation that we all must follow to be in the 'now word'. I whole-heartedly agree that we need to be open to fresh new insights concerning the word of God, new ways of practicing our faith and even new innovative ways of fulfilling the Great Commission. However, what I am addressing is the problem of being *'tossed by fads'* or carried to extremes by *'winds of doctrine'*.

A few questions we can ask are, "Does the teaching bring me into a deeper relationship with the Father through Christ?" "Does it lead me to freedom in Christ by faith?" "Does it help me to identify with the cross and all that was accomplished through the death, burial and resurrection of Christ?" "Does it help me in fulfilling the will of God for my life and being more conformed into the image of Christ?" "Does it help me in fulfilling the Great Commission?" These questions are not exhaustive, but I am simply making a point that it is healthy to ask questions and not follow without thinking for ourselves.

Jude the apostle "felt the necessity to write" the early church which was being influenced by false teaching, and to appeal to them that they contend earnestly for the faith which was once for all delivered to the saints (Jude 1:3). The faith... "delivered to the saints" is the apostolic teaching given believers in the earliest days of the church. We find this foundation outlined in Hebrews 6:1-2 the most basic teachings establishing us in Christ. Yes, we need to move on to maturity, but not before being solidly grounded.

We actually never leave our foundation, but once being equipped we then are able to labor in the grace of God and build our lives with a solid footing. I have seen far too many believers move on before being grounded and they spend their time being '*tossed and blown*' instead of bearing fruit.

Anything that leads us away from the foundation of a relationship with the Lord Jesus Christ is harmful to our spiritual lives. It is only by staying true to the established foundation of Jesus Christ that we can live healthy and productive lives as Christians. Remember we are Christians because we remain Christ centered. He is the 'all in all'.

> [8]"In The church today there are a number of doctrines that have grown bigger than their scriptural proportions and tend to obscure our vision of Christlikeness. Spiritual warfare and deliverance have become for some, doctrinal winds that blow them off course. For others, teachings about personal prosperity, spiritual manifestations or end- time theologies have turned into unbalanced precepts that easily distract from truth that is in Jesus."

None of these things are bad in themselves, but if our focus becomes imbalanced, we can become distorted in our view, which can be detrimental to our spiritual health. [8]"A genuine stirring of God's Spirit, either through a fresh doctrinal understanding or through unique spiritual manifestations, should empower us toward conformity to Christ." The only way we can keep from being imbalanced is by keeping our undivided attention on Christ who is our wisdom and life.

I don't want to be nor do I want you to be one of those people who hunt heresies, but we don't want to be naïve and follow a certain teaching or minister just because it is popular. The U.S.

government trains its people who are looking for counterfeit dollars to become very familiar with real dollar bills. Whatever we worship we are going to be changed into that image. I want to encourage us all to spend our time embracing the worship of our Father and being washed in His soundness of truth. If we do that, then when we are confronted with deception or distortions and extremes due to over emphasizing a particular truth, it will be obvious.

The reality of the word of God is that our main purpose as a part of the kingdom of priests is to become more like Christ so that we can touch this world with love, mercy and power. If we are not reaching the lost and making disciples, then we are missing the main thing. True faith is more than just having sound doctrines; it is abiding in Christ. This does not replace the importance of sound doctrine, nor receiving fresh revelation which we daily need, but true faith is an active pursuit of the Father's heart and doing His will.

A Faithful Bride

During the end of the age we are going to see all human systems shake. Communism, socialism, capitalism, fascism and any other "- ism" are going to fail, since man's wisdom can only take us so far. At the same time, God is going to be actively involved in judging the Babylonian system, which has seduced the nations.

Paul said that he counted all things rubbish so that he may know Christ (Phil. 3:8). As one minister has commented accurately, education is useful when it is put into its proper place. Since Paul called all things rubbish, then we can view education like manure, which is simply good fertilizer that will strengthen and accelerate our understanding.

The older I get, the more I realize no one can figure out all the mysteries of life or even grasp all that is in the Bible; we only learn to walk by faith. We see in part and know in part, and it is for this reason we need fellowship with the body because *we are just a part and the life of wisdom is found in the cluster.*

God's plans are far bigger than our little minds can comprehend. We have the privilege in our days to acquire great amounts of knowledge both secular and biblical, but we need to pray for wisdom. The wise men of Babylon had immense knowledge, but it was the descending wisdom of God that brought answers in a time of need to fulfill God's purpose through Daniel's humility and dependence upon the Spirit. Wisdom is the ability to apply knowledge at the proper time. Knowledge by itself creates pride (I Cor. 8:1), which divides, but wisdom creates dependence on the Spirit, bringing unity.

Jesus is coming back for a bride, not a whore. A bride is faithful and can be trusted. In Ezekiel chapter 16, we see the prophet speak in a graphic way concerning Israel. "When I passed by you and saw you squirming in your blood, I said to you while you were in your blood, Live! I said to you while you were in your blood, 'Live!'" (Ezekiel 16:6). He then goes on to tell the story of how when they had grown up and became prosperous, they did not stay faithful as a wife, but chased after power and idolatry.

We can see in this chapter that the things they were chasing after God used to bring judgment into their lives. The power and riches had corrupted their allegiance to their husband. They had been distracted by so many things, which broke their covenant relationship with God. Remember, it was Samson's comfort with sin, which was his downfall.

Jesus said that the heart is the issue. Adultery, as defined by Jesus, is a heart problem. Covetousness is a heart issue, for where your treasure is, there your heart will also be. I am not just talking about physical adultery, but spiritual adultery, allowing things to take the place of Christ in our lives.

In using the illustration between a man and woman who have experienced one partner's unfaithfulness, it is understood that they can't fix each other's hearts. It takes repentance and turning back to the covenant.

In Ezekiel 16:60, we see the prophet turn Israel back to the covenant of love. In the same way, Jesus told the church in Ephesus to return to their first love and to their first deeds (Revelation 2:4-5). Do you remember when you first received Christ in your heart? The fire of the Holy Spirit consumed you. You could not get enough of the word of God, and you had an obedient heart to listen to the Spirit and reach out to others. What happened to the inward passion and outflowing of love to others? Being the bride of Christ is about cultivating undivided attention on Christ, our husband. Paul said:

> "I am jealous for you with a godly jealousy; for I betrothed you to one husband, that to Christ I might present you as a pure virgin.

But I am afraid, lest as the serpent deceived by his craftiness, your minds should be led astray from simplicity and purity of devotion to Christ." (I Corinthians 11:2-3)

The word "simplicity" means the opposite of "duplicity", which you could call double-minded. James said a double-minded man is unstable because he does not have his heart completely fixed (James 1:8). Paul spoke in a similar manner. He said he did not want the body, or bride, to be tossed about "by every wind of doctrine, by the trickery of men, by craftiness in deceitful scheming; but speaking the truth (holding to or walking in) love, we are to grow up in all aspects into Him, who is the head, even Christ." (Ephesians 4:14-15) *The end of the age is going to bring the church back to its first love of being consumed with Christ Himself.*

Paul whom I am sure we would all consider the apostle that we look to as understanding the purpose of the church had some deep things to say, but he was always brining us into a deeper dependence on Christ our head; not man. He simply wanted to lay foundations, from which, the church would stay grounded and grow so that when he moved on, the saints would be grounded in Christ.

Paul said to the Ephesians elders that "I did not shrink from declaring to you anything that was profitable, and teaching you *publicly* (macro church) and from *house to house* (micro church), solemnly testifying to both Jews and Greeks of repentance toward God and faith in our Lord Jesus Christ." (Acts 20:20-21) Paul laid foundations, but he did not create doctrines of dependence. It is important that we do not create walls to keep people enslaved, dependent or divided from the other parts of the body.

Leadership is for the purpose of liberating. *"Where the Spirit of the Lord is, there is liberty"* (II Corinthians 3:17). True leadership brings freedom to those who are related together under Christ who is our head. Leadership is not for the purpose of dominating, but rather to establish, serve, at times correct and bring the freedom to be all that God has created us to be.

Paul gave us a few signs of false ministries who appear to be 'angels of light'. First, they '*enslave you*' with false teaching or with an over emphasized truth. Then it says, they '*devour you*' or use you for their own benefit. False ministries use people by '*exalting themselves*' over you in a domineering system disguised as spiritual authority.

We can also see from this portion of scripture that they *'take advantage'* of you by demanding or manipulating resources from you. Systems of dependence are the mark of false ministries (II Corinthians 11:13-20). In these systems, maturity is gauged not by your obedience to the simple truth of God's word, but to your obedience to those set over you.

- If you are disobedient, then they will shame you into submission through open humiliation, rejection or manipulation.
- If you are part of such a system, I would encourage you to leave and find a group of loving believers that understand freedom, true fellowship, grace and soundness of truth.

Please don't take what I am saying out of context. I am confronting abuse, but in no way discouraging fellowship, leadership and accountability since teamwork is essential for successful Christian living. It was in this context of dealing with false ministries that Paul talked about being led astray from "simplicity and purity" of devotion to Christ.

SIFTING AND UNION A PROCESS OF THE HARVEST

Christ is our resurrected High Priest at the right hand of the Father and He is the soon returning Husband for His Bride. Once the New Covenant was established Christ then commissioned His bride with His authority to:

"Go therefore and make disciples of all the nations." Matthew 28:20

As I was writing this book, I had certain ideas about what the bride of Christ exemplifies in the word of God, and then as I studied, I discovered a simple yet profound truth. The bride of Christ is about the church returning to her very foundations and I also learned the bride is not supposed to be hiding in her closet praying, but out among the nations making disciples. Yes, the bride is a passionately praying, worshipping company, but we are not to be hidden; rather, we are to be out in the open displaying the light of Christ. When everything is shaking, we return to our foundations and put into practice our faith. The faithful bride is not sitting around waiting, but she is actively working under the power of the Spirit (Prov. 31).

The bride in Revelation 19:8 is clothed "in fine linen, bright and clean; for the fine linen is the righteous acts of the saints." The holy bride wears only fine linen, white and pure, such as the attire of the high priest when he entered annually into the Holy of Holies before the presence of God (Lev. 16:4). In the text of Revelation 19:8, the word 'righteous acts' is actually the word righteousness, and the focus of righteousness is our most basic foundation, the cross. It is out of the cross that flows all of our fellowship with Father and the good works we have been called to accomplish (Ephesians 2:10).

Paul, in Ephesians 5:27, says that the church Christ is returning for will be without "spot or wrinkle or any such thing; but that she should be holy and blameless." The bride of Christ is called to be without spot, which speaks of her purity. The main pathway of our purity or sanctification is the washing of the word of God through the renewing of our minds (Romans 12:1).

It is why having a clear understanding of the truth is of utmost importance in aiding us to be holy in our relationship with God. This correlates with how the priest in the Old Testament had to be ceremonially washed daily before entering into the presence of God in the Tabernacle (Leviticus 14).

In looking at this word *spot* we can see that it refers to a moral blemish. In Jude 1:12, and II Peter 2:13, the reference to moral spots is to false teachers who are stains and blemishes. False teachers spread the cancer of immorality, division, deception and pride through their arrogance, which is simply a *rejection of the cross* (Philippians 3:17-19).

A great separation is coming in the church, which is actually happening in our midst and will become more apparent as the end of the age approaches. It is the fullness of God's judgment in the church (I Peter 4:17) before He begins to judge the nations as revealed in the book of Revelation. Selfish ambition, immorality, self-seeking, financial corruption, and spiritual abuse is being dealt with in the church. Leaders will either repent and be restored to the place of servants, or they will become deceived and deceivers. *The leaders of the bride of Christ are going to be clothed in humility and sacrifice* so that the church will be holy and blameless. Unity produced through humility is a mark of the true church working with one mind and heart to fulfill the original mandate of making disciples.

The Lexical Aids to the New Testament says this word "blameless" in Ephesians 5:27 is actually "a technical word to designate the absence of anything amiss in a sacrifice." *The church is going to give itself to bring salvation to a dying world at the end of the age.* Paul said in Colossians1:24 that, "I rejoice in my sufferings for your sake, and in my flesh I do my share on behalf of His body (which is the church) in filling up that which is lacking in Christ's afflictions." It was not that Paul could add to the cross, but by dedicating himself to the cross, through his life others could be touched. The bride will be openly displaying the redemptive work of the cross in love, good works and power. Psalm 110:3 say's "thy people will be free-will offerings in the day of thy power".

"The bride will be without wrinkle" signifies the church's youthfulness and unity. As we return to our foundations we will see eye to eye (Isaiah 52:8) because we are all beholding the resurrected Christ. As we come to Zion, the city of God, or the place of God's presence we will begin to see in unison, since we are established on the same unshakable foundation (I Peter 2:6-7). The only place the word 'wrinkle' is actually found in the Bible is Ephesians 5:27. A faithful bride will be undistracted in the midst of the confusion of the end of the age, since it will take undivided attention to complete our purpose.

The bride of Christ is a message of returning to the foundation of the threshing floor where covenant is established. As I previously wrote, "the threshing floor" was symbolic of the relationship between the bride and the bridegroom. It is not insignificant that Ruth came to Boaz at the 'threshing floor' (Ruth 3:6-14). Boaz represents Christ (our kinsman-redeemer) and Ruth, the bride of Christ. At the center of the threshing floor, one finds two large flat stones, one resting on the top of the other. They were fitted and joined together. The top stone was known as the female and the bottom stone the male. The grinding of grain was a depiction of the act of marriage (Job 31:10). The symbolism represents the union that we must embrace with Christ along with the fulfilling of our purpose by being one mind and heart, united in fulfilling the Great Commission.

PRUDENCE FULFILLS THE MISSION

Let's take a look at the words of Christ. In Matthew's gospel, right after Jesus finished talking about His return and the signs of the end of the age, He tells several parables. We are all familiar with the parable of the ten virgins the five *prudent* ones had oil and were ready. In Matthew 7:24, Jesus talked about the **prudent** man who heard the words of Christ and applied them in governing or building his life. In Matthew 24:45, Jesus talked about the **prudent** slave who was alert and faithful not distracted. Then in Luke 16, Jesus commends a man for his **prudence** in dealing with the affairs of this world. He then makes a profound statement, connecting our spirituality to how we deal with money or possessions. Jesus was telling us that we can possess finances as long as they don't possess us. It boils down to worship! You cannot worship money and God at the same time, but you can be a steward of money, which will actually reflect your worship of the Father.

If you go and study all of these parables that relate to Christ coming back for His bride you will see the word *prudence,* or wisdom. The word found in all of the above scriptures is the Greek word *phronimos*, which means 'practically wise in relationships with others'. In looking at Christ's return, we many times spiritualize everything, but as I have shown you that as New Covenant priests, there is a practical side to our faith.

Application is who we really are, not what we say. You can claim your faithfulness to Christ all day long, but how do you act. Do you display faithfulness? You may be real faithful in your prayer closet, but what happens when you are confronted with sin or pressure? Are you filled with the Spirit? Then you will not only have power, but a heart of compassion, kindness, humility, gentleness and patience. You will forgive, put up with each other and not complain, but walk in unity (Colossians 3:12-14). The prudent remain faithful to Christ and His body at all times because they have committed themselves completely to the cross. Application is where the rubber meets the word. Our worship is displayed in both our inward thoughts and outward actions; it is holistic, encompassing every detail of our lives.

The bride is going to be an overcoming company of believers. In the midst of great darkness, the Spirit is going to lift up a standard. The first three chapters of Revelation give us many promises to those who overcome. It is in Revelation 12:11 that we are told how to overcome. It says:

"They overcame him because of the blood of the Lamb and because of the word of their testimony, and they did not love their life even unto death."

The same author wrote, "For whatever is born of God overcomes the world; and this is the victory that has overcome the world – our faith" (I John 5:4). I don't know what this overcoming bride is going to look like, but I do know that we have been commissioned to use the power and wisdom of God to bring restoration to a world without hope.

The bride is going to be clothed with fine linen garments. The linen garments are symbolic of an active bride laboring in the ability of the Spirit. To apply the scriptures in our own strength is nothing, but religion. The bride must live from the new creation life of the Spirit, but she must do good works. Faith without application is dead (James 2:20).

If we have faith, then we are going to minister to those in need. Yes, we are going to be faithful in prayer and praise, worshipping the Father in spirit and truth, but we are also going to be moved with compassion for the hurting of this world. We are going to have boldness to preach the word of God and lay down our lives if necessary to the point of death, but we are also going to be willing to lay our lives down for others. Jesus said that the love of many would grow cold and it is for this reason that we are told to encourage one another (Hebrews 10:24) to love and good works.

As I have already said in this book, I don't propose to have all the answers nor is this an exhaustive interpretation of Revelation. I am looking at trends in the world happening, so that we can navigate through the times in which we live. It seems that almost every generation has thought that they would be those who would see the return of Christ. I am not going to be so presumptuous to think that our generation is the one, but I can confidently say that we are closer than we have ever been before. The one thing of which we can be certain is where our focus should be. Our complete focus needs to be our covenant relationship with Christ. Great darkness is covering the face of the earth, but the manifest presence of the Spirit is going to rest upon those who are dedicated to seeing Him who is high and lifted up.

In contrast to the Babylonian system at the end of this present age, there is going to be a bride in the earth totally dedicated to her husband. On a personal level, are you totally dedicated to Christ as your husband? Do you spend time being washed in His word and having intimate communion with Him? Do you desire to be closer to him than to the many distractions Babylon presents to you? Is His life reaching out through you to a hurting world? You can only be assured to make it through these deceptive days and especially the difficulties of the end of the age if you are totally dedicated to your heavenly Husband Christ our very foundation.

Appendix A

Methods for Interpreting the Book of Revelation

The first method of interpretation I want to look at is the **preterist** method. In this interpretive approach to the book of Revelation, it is taught that the symbols and content relate only to events and happenings at the time when the book was written. It is taught that the beast of chapter 13, for example, related entirely to Rome or some say specifically identified Nero Caesar during the first century. The 'city of Rome' and the Imperial priesthood are seen as the Babylonian whore of Revelation 14, 17 and 18. An alternative view is that the Babylonian whore is to be identified with Jerusalem and the Jewish system of worship. However, both views sees no future prophetic content in the book of Revelation whatsoever, except for the return of Christ to the earth.

Preterist tend to take the postmillennial view of the 1,000 year reign of Christ. The view sees the millennial reign of Christ in Revelation 20 as not a literal 1,000 years but a symbol of completeness. It is an undetermined amount of time during this age, when Christ is going to rule the nations through the church. It is a belief that the enemies of Christ will be put under the feet of the church ruling the nations during this age. It is a view that the body of believers conquers the whole world for the gospel, and the entire world acknowledges Christ. Then, at the end of the millennial reign of Christ, He will physically return to setup a new heaven and new earth.

Great men of God in the history of the church have taken this view, such as Charles Finney and Jonathan Blanchard (the founder of Wheaton College). During the 1980's and 1990's in America, many Charismatic ministers began to embrace parts of this theology, which became known as the "Kingdom Now Movement". Around twenty percent of this movement embraces the postmillennial position while the majority within the movement embraces Amillennialism.

Preterist Authors:
J. Marcellus Kik, "An Eschatology of Victory"
David Chilton, "The Days of Vengeance"

The second method of interpretation is known as the **idealist or symbolic** method. The church father, Augustine, held this view, and it was the predominant view until the Protestant Reformation. In this understanding, the contents of the book of Revelation are not seen to relate to any historical events at all, but only to symbolize the ongoing struggle between good and evil during the church age until Christ returns. In general, the idealist view is marked by a refusal to identify any of the images with specific future events, whether in the history of the church or with regard to the end of all things.

The primary benefit of this view is that it renders the book of Revelation quite understandable at a basic level. It is simply a book that was written to encourage suffering saints in the knowledge that God will someday conquer all evil and make things right.

Idealists are amillennial in their view of Revelation 20 concerning the millennial reign of Christ. [10]"Amillennial means "no literal Millennium." Some people would rather call this view present-millennialism."

Amillennialism holds that while Christ's reign during the millennium is spiritual in nature, at the end of the church age, Christ will return in final judgment and establish the new heavens and new earth. Amillennialism has been the predominant view of believers during the history of the church among Catholics, Lutherans, Reformed, and many of the original Baptists. This view has predominantly been popular among covenant theologians. The majority of the "Kingdom Now" proponents tend to be amillennial or they combine the postmillennial and amillennial position of the millennial reign of Christ together.

Idealist Authors:
Oswald Allis, "Prophecy and the Church"
Leon Morris, "The Revelation of Saint John"

The third method I want to look at is the **historicist** method of interpretation. The majority of the Protestant reformers interpreted the Revelation in this way. In this understanding of the book, the events describe actual events from the beginning of the church until the time of the interpreter.

The Protestant reformers could say that the Catholic pope was the Antichrist and the Catholic Church was Babylon. In this view, Revelation was interpreted in the light of the history of Western Europe through the various popes, the Protestant Reformation, the French Revolution, and individual leaders such as Charlemagne or Napoleon. In unison, just about all of the Protestant Reformers such as Luther, Calvin and Zwingli took this position.

Historicists vary in their interpretive approach and none of them agree as to how history and scripture correlate. It does make the book relevant to every generation of believers. Today those taking the historicist view have varying interpretations of the millennial reign of Christ.

Historicist Authors:
William Hendiksen, "More than Conquerors"
Steve Wohlberg, "End Time Delusions"

The fourth method of dealing with Revelation is the **dispensational futurist** or known as 'Dispensational Theology'. Dispensationalism is the most known and popular method in America. Dispensationalism divides the Bible into seven time periods, it is claimed that God's saving activity is organized differently in each. One of the teachings of Dispensationalism is that the present age will end with a terrible seven-year manifestation of the wrath of God upon the whole earth. However, the true church will not partake of this tribulation, for immediately prior to it, Christ will have secretly come and taken the saints away to heaven. This coming, it is taught, may occur at any moment. The teaching is that Christ first comes for the church then comes back to the world after the seven-year tribulation period.

'The Left Behind' fiction series co-authored by Tim LaHaye and Jerry B. Jenkins is based on this interpretation. The series has popularized this method. The method relies heavily upon the distinction between Israel and the church and the distinctive plan God has for both. This view teaches that Revelation Chapter 4 is the rapture of the church, which is a secret event and the rest of the book is exclusively dealing with national Israel. God's people in Revelation are Israel, restored to Jerusalem with a rebuilt temple where the Antichrist sets up his image for the world to worship.

The church does not return to the earth until Revelation 19 at Christ's return to the earth.

Dispensationalist and moderate futurist agree on the premillenial position on Revelation 20. It is believed that Jesus Christ will literally return to the Mt. of Olives and reign on the earth for one thousand years. All moderate futurists do not take the position that it necessarily has to be literally one thousand years, but an indefinite period of time. It will be the physical reign of Christ on this earth from the nation of Israel along with the resurrected saints from all ages.

Dispensational Authors:
Clarence Larkin, "The Book of Revelation"
John Walvrood, "The Revelation of Jesus Christ"

The fifth method is referred to as a **moderate futurist** or the historic premillenial view. George Ladd has popularized this view, and it is a departure from the Dispensational view. Moderate futurism finds no reason to cut the cord between Israel and the church. The primary purpose of the Revelation is to describe the consummation of this present age, which includes the church, Israel and the nations.

The view sees the rapture of the church and the return of Christ as one event at the consummation of the age. At the same time the view incorporates the preterist interpretation, which is simply a foreshadowing of the final consummation.

The moderate futurist sees aspects of the idealist view by seeing many aspects of the Revelation as symbolically reflecting the ongoing struggle between the kingdom of God and the enemies of Christ. In addition, it sees the historical judgment of Jerusalem by the Roman armies like the preterist, but merely as a foreshadowing of the final appearance of the Antichrist kingdom at the end of the age. To the moderate futurist Rome was a type or historical figure of the final Antichrist and his short attempt to rule that is yet to appear in the future.

The historic premillenial position believes that the kingdom is presently at work in the earth through the church, but also not yet fully manifested; they believe that the kingdom is in the midst of the world as a witness during this age. It sees the church as 'salt and light' in a wicked world, while at the end of this transitional age, Jesus will return which includes a catching away of the living saints and the resurrection of the saints who have died (I Thess. 4:16-17). We will meet Him in the air, after a brief complex series of events, which will culminate in the return of Jesus with His saints to set up a one thousand-year rule on earth with Christ as 'King of kings'. During the millennial reign of Christ both Israel and the nations will embrace Jesus Christ as King and Savior, since Israel will be the capital of the nations in that age.

Moderate Futurist Authors:
George Ladd, "A Commentary on the Revelation of John"
Dan Juster and Keith Intrader, "Israel, The Church and The Last Days"

Conclusion:

I have purposely tried to keep this information simple enough for any reader. I am giving you an over simplification of each method, but this is the basic premise of each. What you will find are many writers, which blend several of the methods together. If you want to get more details on each one of these views I recommend doing your own study of this subject by getting the suggested books of each view.

Each view has its own merit, and much can be gleaned from each. Solid scholars are positioned in each camp and we should never break fellowship over our positions. I personally see validation for each view and tend to pick from the best of all the methods.

BIBLIOGRAPHY

1. "Unfinished Business" by Greg Ogden, Zondervan, 2003 pg. 18.

2. "Unfinished Business" by Greg Ogden, Zondervan, 2003 pg. 62.

3. "Unfinished Business" by Greg Ogden, Zondervan, 2003 pg. 52.

4. "Team Leadership in Christian Ministry" by Kenneth O. Gangel, Moody Press, 1997 Pg. 35-36.

5. "God's Judgements" by Mark A. Noll, Intervarsity Press, 2007. Pg. 17.

Chapter 1

1. "Created For Worship" by Noel Due, Mentor Imprint, 2005 pg. 41.

2. "The More Excellent Ministry" by Kelly Varner, Destiny Image, 1988 pg. 52,

3. "Created For Worship" by Noel Due, Mentor Imprint, 2005 pg. 41.

4. "Kingdom Come" by John Wimber, (Ann Arbor, Michigan: Vine Books), Pg. 14, 16, 29.

5. "The Parabolic Teaching of Scripture" by G.H. Lang, (Grand Rapids, Michigan), Pg. 19.

6. "The Gospel of the Kingdom" by George E. Ladd, (Grand Rapids, Michigan), Pg. 17, 101.

7. "We Become What We Worship" by G.K. Beale, Intervarsity Press, 2008 Pg. 166.

8. "Created For Worship" by Noel Due, Mentor Imprint, 2005 pg. 156.

9. "Our Father Abraham" by Marvin R. Wilson, Wm. B. Eerdmans Publishing Co, 1989 Pg. 176.

10. "God's Judgements" by Mark A. Noll, Intervarsity Press, 2007. Pg. 17.

11. "God's Judgements" by Mark A. Noll, Intervarsity Press, 2007. Pg. 78.

Chapter 2

1. "Our Father Abraham" by Marvin R. Wilson, Wm. B. Eerdmans Publishing Co, 1989 Pg. 267.

2. George E. Ladd, "The Gospel of the Kingdom", (Grand Rapids, Michigan), Pg. 36.

3. James Jacob Prasch, "Midrash", Moriel Ministries, 2009 pg. 8.

4. "Created For Worship" by Noel Due, Mentor Imprint, 2005 pg. 63-64.

5. "The Days of His Presence" by Francis Frangipane, Arrow Publications, 1995 pg. 81.

6. "Roaring Lambs", by Bob Briner, Zondervan 1993, Pg. 47-48.

7. "When Jesus Returns", by David Pawson, Hodder & Stroughton, 1995, Pg. 148.

8. "Global Socially" by Robin Cohen & Paul Kennedy", New York University Press, 2000, Pg. 24.

9. "Unveiling Empire" by Wes Howard-Brook and Anthony Gwyther, Orbis Books, 2005, Pg. 238, 252.

10. "The Ecstasy of Loving God" by John Crowder, Destiny Image , 2009, Pg. 47.

11. "The Days of His Presence" by Francis Frangipane, Arrow Publications, 1995 pg. 128.

Chapter 3

1. "Created For Worship" by Noel Due, Mentor Imprint, 2005 pg. 134.

2. "One New Man", Reuvon Doron, Embrace 1993, Pg. 19-20.

3. "The Spirit of Truth", Arthur Katz & Paul Volk, Morning Star Publications, 1993, Pg 64.

4. "The Spirit of Truth", Arthur Katz & Paul Volk, Morning Star Publications, 1993, Pg 95.

5. "Revolution" by George Barana, Barna Group, 2005.

6. "Beware of Spiritual Wolves" by Roger Sapp, All Nations Publications, Pg. 3.

7. "Imagine: A Vision For Christians In The Arts", Steve Turner, InterVasity Press, 2001, Pg. 44.

8. "The Prophetic Song", by LaMar Boschman, Revival Press, 1992 Pg. 53.

Chapter 4

1. "Training the Laity for Ministry" by Robert Munger, Theology News and Notes (June 1973), Pg. 3.

2. "Unfinished Business" by Greg Ogden, Zondervan, 2003 pg. 101.

3. "Rethinking the Wineskin" by Frank Viola, Present Testimony Ministry 2001, Pg. 36.

4. "The Habitation of God" by Rick Joyner, Morning Star Journal, Vol 3, No. 3, Pg. 44.

Chapter 5

1. "The Clash of Civilizations and the Remaking of World Order" by Samuel Huntington, Touchstone 1996 pg. 106.

2. "Orissa Braces for More Hindu-Christian Conflict" by Michelle A. Vu, Christian Post Today, Nov. 10, 2008.

3. "Putin's Reunited Russia" by Yuri ZarKhoVich, Time Magazine, May 17, 2007.

4. "At Expense of All Others Putin Picks A Church" by Clifford Jay Levy, New York Times, April 24, 2008.

5. "The Clash of Civilizations and the Remaking of World Order" by Samuel Huntington, Touchstone 1996 pg. 106.

6. "Britain's War on Christianity: America's Future Fight?" by Dale Hurd, CBN Online, July 28, 2009.

7. "Created For Worship" by Noel Due, Mentor Imprint, 2005 pg. 27.

8. "The Days of His Presence" by Francis Frangipane, Arrow Publications, 1995, pg. 95-96.

9. "Created For Worship" by Noel Due, Mentor Imprint, 2005 pg. 29.

10. "Israel, The Church and The Last Days" by Dan Juster and Keith Intrader, Destiny Image, 2003 pg. 65.

www.ingramcontent.com/pod-product-compliance
Lightning Source LLC
Chambersburg PA
CBHW072025040426
42447CB00009B/1731